Bl
2.00

D0888365

W7-CGR-141

DISCARDED
UNIVER   NPEG
PORTAGE & BALMORAL
WINNIPEG 2, MAN.   CANADA

The Critical Idiom
General Editor: JOHN D. JUMP

4 *The Conceit*

PR
535
·M37R8

The Conceit/*K. K. Ruthven*

Methuen & Co Ltd

First published 1969
by Methuen & Co Ltd
11 New Fetter Lane London EC4
© 1969 K. K. Ruthven
Printed in Great Britain
by Cox & Wyman Ltd Fakenham Norfolk

SBN   416   15730   0   Hardback
SBN   416   15740   8   Paperback

*This is available in both hardback and paperback
editions. The paperback edition is sold subject to the
condition that it shall not, by way of trade or
otherwise, be lent re-sold, hired out, or otherwise
circulated without the publisher's prior consent in
any form other than that in which it is published
and without a similar condition being imposed on
the subsequent purchaser.*

*Distributed in the U.S.A.
by Barnes & Noble Inc.*

To SIMON *and* GUY
disturbers of the piece

Contents

General Editor's Preface

This volume is one of a series of short studies, each dealing with a single key item, or a group of two or three key items, in our critical vocabulary. The purpose of the series differs from that served by the standard glossaries of literary terms. Many terms are adequately defined for the needs of students by the brief entries in these glossaries, and such terms will not be the subjects of studies in the present series. But there are other terms which cannot be made familiar by means of compact definitions. Students need to grow accustomed to them through simple and straightforward but reasonably full discussions of them. The purpose of the present series is to provide such discussions.

Some of the terms in question refer to literary movements (e.g. 'Romanticism', 'Aestheticism', etc.), others to literary kinds (e.g. 'Comedy', 'Epic', etc.), and still others to stylistic features (e.g. 'Irony', 'The Conceit', etc.). Because of this diversity of subject-matter, no attempt has been made to impose a uniform pattern upon the studies. But all authors have tried to provide as full illustrative quotation as possible, to make reference whenever appropriate to more than one literature, in more than a single language, and to compose their studies in such a way as to guide readers towards the short bibliographies in which they have made suggestions for further reading.

John D. Jump

University of Manchester

I

The Word 'Conceit'

A generation ago it was proposed that we should stop using the word *conceit* because it had acquired far too many meanings to be of help as a literary term. At the moment it is still circulating freely, especially in books and articles on sixteenth- and seventeenth-century poetry, and we are no nearer to establishing its precise meaning now than we were in 1941 when Potter registered his protest against the term. Certainly it is used to cover an extraordinary range of poetic phenomena. If a poet compares his mistress' eyes to stars and her teeth to pearls we say he is using conceits, and if he composes little anecdotes about her escapades with Cupid or explains how her presence makes the flowers bloom we again call these things conceits; it is also a conceit to speak of the freezing fires of love, to compare an elegist's pen to a waterspout and lovers to a pair of compasses, to refer to the wound in Christ's side as a wardrobe and to Christ's shroud as a handkerchief. A mere catalogue of conceits would form a substantial book.

During the years when conceits of one sort or another were practically the staple of English poetry, the word *conceit* possessed a variety of meanings which made it fruitfully ambiguous in the hands of a poet. At the end of the sixteenth century it was still being used (as Chaucer had used it) as a synonym for *thought* and in predominantly non-poetic contexts where the customary word nowadays would be something like *concept, conception* or *idea*; but it was also applied to such diverse things as a completely unfounded supposition, a witty remark or idea, a clever act of deception, and the products of the artistic imagination. There were reputable conceits which philosophers trafficked in, and disreputable conceits on which old wives' tales were nourished; and somewhere between these extremes lay literary conceits, which are neither logically verifiable in the way that philosophical conceits are, nor childishly superstitious in the manner of old wives' tales, nor socially undesirable like the activities of a confidence trickster. There were also witty conceits which might take the form of an emblem or an armorial device, and there were poetic conceits which resulted from an attempt to domicile the Italian *concetto* in England. A person who used conceits might be anything from a fool or a charlatan to a genius. It was all very confusing.

The semantic drift from *thought* to *a witty thought* seems not to have occurred before the sixteenth century, and it was not until the following century that *wit* (in the modern sense) became a dominant element in *conceit*. The fluctuation in meaning is reflected in the titles of various books published in the period. It is uncertain whether the 'book of conceits' mentioned in a 1550 inventory for Ely House was a collection of aphorisms or a collection of witticisms, although it is likely to have been the former, and highly unlikely to have been a collection of poetic conceits. *The Wellspring of Witty Conceits* (1584) is an anthology of aphorisms, and the subtitle of Robert Hitchcock's *The Quintessence of Wit* (1590) advertises the book as 'a current comfort of conceits, maxims, and politic devices'. Gervase Markham's *Conceited Letters* (1618) is a guide to letter-writing, but *The Mirror of Mirth and Pleasant Conceits* (1583) aligns conceits with jest-book material in a manner that was becoming habitual by the time Randolph wrote *The Conceited Pedlar* (1630).

Shakespeare hardly ever uses *conceit* as we use it nowadays in expressions like *sonneteering conceits*, and in this he is typical of his age. He seems to approach the modern usage in presenting an altercation between a Yorkist and a Lancastrian on the moral symbolism of red roses and white roses (*I Henry VI*, IV i 89–107), but the meaning of *conceit* in this passage is ambiguous. There is a less dubious example in *Titus Andronicus*, in the episode where Titus sends the men who have raped and mutilated his daughter 'a bundle of weapons, and verses writ upon them', the verses being Horace's lines about how the man of upright life needs neither bow nor javelin. The appropriateness of Titus' symbolic gesture is appreciated by Aaron, who describes it as a 'conceit' which 'our witty empress' would have applauded (IV ii 29 f.); and here, for once, Shakespeare and his modern critics seem to be using *conceit* in almost the same way. Isolated examples of the modern usage occur elsewhere, as in Greene's *Never Too Late* (1590), where Insida warbles out a 'conceited ditty' which is a catalogue of Petrarchan conceits (*Works*, ed. Grosart, VIII 74 f.); but the fact is that most Elizabethans tended to use some other word altogether, like *device* or *invention*, when referring to what we would call literary conceits. William Webbe, for instance, calls Skelton 'a pleasant conceited fellow, and of a very sharp wit', but refers to the products of such wit as 'rare devices and singular inventions of poetry', not rare and singular conceits (*Discourse* (1586), pp. 33, 35); and Thomas Watson, whose *Hekatompathia* (1582) is stiff with conceits in our sense of the word, invariably uses *invention* where we would use *conceit*, as when he praises Serafino's 'many pretty inventions concerning the looking-glass of his mistress' (xxiii). When the word *conceit* was used in connection with poetry it tended to be used in the singular and to mean the idea *for* a poem rather than the ideas or metaphors *in* a poem. This explains why many of the pieces in Nicolas Breton's *Melancholic Humours* (1600) do not contain many familiar conceits despite the fact that they bear titles like 'A Solemn Conceit', 'A Farewell to Conceit' and 'An Odd Conceit' (the original spelling is *conceipt*, but the form *conceited* occurs in another poem called 'A Conceited Fancy', where *conceited* means *witty*). Probably, therefore, we misunderstand the subtitle of the second edition of Constable's *Diana*

(1594) – 'the excellent conceitful sonnets of H.C.' – if we take it to mean that the poems in this volume are full of sonneteering conceits. On the contrary, I think it was meant to inform potential buyers that Constable's poems display a high degree of imaginative conception and are worth having on that account, as are the 'sweet conceited sonnets' in Spenser's *Amoretti* (1595) or 'the sweet conceits of Philip Desportes' (Lodge, *A Margarite of America* (1596): *Works*, iii 79).

The identification of *conceit* with *concetto* ought to be illuminating, but it is not, because the Italian word was equally as ambiguous as the English one, and could mean 'concept, idea, image, an intuition of analogy, a pungent statement, a witty metaphor, or any witty figure of thought or sound' (Mirollo, p. 116). As the Spanish *concepto* is similarly unhelpful, we are unlikely to get very far by comparing *conceit* with its European equivalents. It is more profitable to investigate the theory of conceits, for there we find a common set of assumptions about the nature and function of metaphor from which Spain derived its *conceptismo*, Italy its *concettismo* and England its 'conceited style'.

2

The Theoretical
Basis of Conceits

ORNAMENT OR INSIGHT?

'Aristotle could be regarded as the father of the conceit' says
Duncan in his book on the revival of Metaphysical poetry (p. 10),
and Mazzeo reports that *conceit* and *metaphor* are synonymous terms
in *seicento* criticism (p. 30). The reason for this is that the kind of
metaphor Aristotle discusses is what Milton classifies as a 'disjunct
similitude' (*similitudo disjuncta*) in which all four terms of a comparison are distinguished separately (*Artis Logicae*, I xxi); and a
disjunct similitude, with its emphasis on proportion and reciprocity
of parts, resembles the cognitive metaphors of Metaphysical poetry
far more closely than the evocative metaphors of Romantic and
Symbolist poetry. 'When B is to A as D is to C, then instead of B
the poet will say D and B instead of D' (*Poetics*, 1457^b11). It all
sounds very mechanical, and so it is, after the initial act of noticing
the hidden similarity between B and D has taken place; but the
point is that very few people have 'an intuitive perception of the
similarity in dissimilars', which is why Aristotle identifies metaphor as the hall-mark of genius (*Poetics*, 1459^a17). Donne's
'spider love, which transubstantiates all, And can convert manna
to gall' ('Twickenham Garden') is a brilliantly illuminating conceit
which illustrates the importance of perception in the yoking of such
opposites as *spider* and *love*. Aristotle here talks about metaphor
as a process rather than a commodity, as a mode of perception and
not a literary ornament. For although you can teach someone to
make the most of a hidden similarity between a certain B and D

once he has noticed it, and even train him to be on the look-out for similarities in other *B*s and *D*s, you cannot teach the act of perception itself. Perception is not a literary technique but an act of the mind which a great poet shares with a great scientist or a great philosopher. It is therefore to this section of the *Poetics* that critics turn whenever it is necessary to defend far-fetched conceits or explain their heuristic function as speculative instruments.

In classical rhetoric, on the other hand, emphasis is placed mainly on the ornamental value of metaphor in adorning an already existent perception. 'We make use of metaphors . . . that are appropriate', says Aristotle (*Rhetoric*, 1405^{a}9), for these are what give 'clearness, charm and distinction' to writing; and this is the attitude taken by Cicero, who treats metaphor in his *De Oratore* (III xlii) as 'a valuable stylistic ornament' (*magnum ornamentum orationis*) which orators are advised to cultivate because, as Quintilian says, 'it adds to the copiousness of language' (*Institutio Oratoria*, VIII vi 4). This is very different from saying that metaphor is a way of looking. It also lowers the status of metaphor, as the perceptual metaphors of men of genius will be obviously superior to the ornamental metaphors of bright undergraduates in an academy for rhetoricians; and it is curious that Aristotle should not have perceived this and dissociated the two functions of metaphor more clearly. Metaphor-as-ornament is a teachable concept and so it became the dominant one, while the eclipse of metaphor-as-insight made it easier for enemies of the conceited style in poetry to make their slanders stick. *Ornamental* is too easily interpreted to mean *merely ornamental* or even *superfluously ornamental*, and if metaphors are treated habitually as the garment of style it is only a matter of time before people start proclaiming the virtues of walking naked.

In our own century the idea that metaphor can be either a decoration or a way of looking has influenced our way of describing and evaluating the conceited poetry of the English Renaissance. Our

terms are not Aristotelian, but our distinction is. Instead of disso-
ciating the perceptual from the ornamental we have separated the
functional from the decorative, Metaphysical conceits from sonneteering conceits, the unconventional from the trite, the seventeenth
century from the sixteenth, great rooted blossomers from flowers
stuck in sand. It is impressively tidy and schematic, and perhaps
even accurate, although Rosemond Tuve's book on the continuity
of sixteenth- and seventeenth-century poetic techniques casts
doubts on that score. What is amazing is that we have been able to
create an influential critical principle as well as a literary-historical
concept of period out of what was merely a rhetorical distinction
in antiquity between the act of thinking and the expression of
thought.

'DISCORDIA CONCORS'

Whereas ancient rhetoricians were preoccupied with metaphor-as-
ornament, modern critics concentrate on metaphor-as-insight and
probe into the emotions generated by what Coleridge once called
'the balance or reconciliation of opposite or discordant qualities'
(*Biographia Literaria* (1817), ch. xiv). He was probably recollect-
ing Johnson's analysis of Metaphysical wit as 'a kind of *discordia
concors*; a combination of dissimilar images, or discovery of occult
resemblances in things apparently unlike' (*Lives of the Poets*
(1779): Cowley), a definition which is fundamental to more recent
analyses of the shock of recognition induced by a skilfully deploy-
ed conceit. Looked at in this way, the conceit is a respectably
ancient mode of thought like the paradox, for the deftly mani-
pulated paradoxes of religious poets testify to the powers of yoked
contraries in evoking ideas which cannot be defined: 'the clerkly
conveying of contraries', as Webbe calls it, has long been recog-
nized as a function of both paradox and conceit (*Discourse* (1586),
p. 65). To spend one's time leaping imaginatively among incompatibles may seem to call for tireless virtuosity in a writer, but the

metaphoric process was probably less exacting in the early seven-teenth century, when analogical modes of thought were at least as familiar as the logical, with the result that what we now think of as being specifically 'poetic' approaches to experience were the com-mon property of divines and professional men as well as poets. Consider, for instance, the once important legal principle of *equiparation*. Kantorowicz defines this as 'the action of placing on equal terms two or more subjects which at first appear to have nothing to do with each other' (p. 362): *aequiparatio* of the Church, a city, and a maniac (to use Kantorowicz's example) rests on the fact that all are technically 'minors' unable to handle their own affairs and consequently in need of guardians. Anybody who is trained to think like that during office hours will find nothing odd in Shakespeare's equiparation of lunatics, lovers and poets on the grounds that they are 'of imagination all compact' (*A Mid-summer Night's Dream*, V i 8). The equiparation of poet and jurist, I am tempted to suggest, is that both are men of wit, hypersensitive to occult resemblances and eagerly delighting in a *discordia concors*.

It was a rhetorician, John Hoskins, who stressed the importance of 'inventing matter of agreement in things most unlike' (and by *inventing* he means *discovering*, not *fabricating*: the connection is 'there' all the time, but one needs acuity of wit in order to perceive it). The blackboard example he gives of such incompatibles is rather feeble: 'London and a tennis court', it turns out, are alike because 'in both all the gain goes to the hazard' (*Directions* (1600), p. 18). Bateson quotes this passage in illustration of what he calls 'the Principle of the Semantic Gap' in poetry, which is this: the more heterogeneous the constituents of a metaphor are, the greater the poet's triumph if a synthesis is achieved (pp. 49–51). By what is semantically a leap of faith the poet crosses the gap and proclaims the compatibility of incompatibles. For him it is a moment of triumph, the satisfaction of a *difficulté vaincue*; for us, his readers, it can be a moment of revelation, an intimation of unsuspected harmony on the far side of disparity.

THE POETIC OF CORRESPONDENCE

When Johnson describes the resemblances in a *discordia concors* as 'occult' he seems to be recalling earlier theories about the transcendental origins of metaphor and the status of conceits in times when the universe was imagined to be a vast net-work of symbolic correspondences. As soon as the material world is seen to be a token of the spiritual, the earth itself becomes the shadow of heaven (*Paradise Lost*, V 574 f.) and literary sacramentalists can spend their lives documenting the theory

> That in this world there's not a wart
> That has not there a counterpart. (*Hudibras*, II iii 227 f.)

Usually they do it less frivolously than Butler's lines suggest, on account of a conviction that the divine message is figured symbolically in created nature as well as set down literally in the Bible. It was commonplace in the Renaissance to speak of the world as 'a universal and public manuscript' (*Religio Medici* (1643), I xvi) containing sermons in stones and books in the running brooks, accessible to anybody with Browne's erudition and the patience of a cryptologist. God himself could be imagined as the archetypal concettist who created a world which St Augustine calls an exquisite poem (*De Civitate Dei*, xi 18), a poem full of occult correspondences, enigmatically impenetrable to undistinguished minds but an immensely rich hieroglyph to connoisseurs of the recondite. If God made poets in his own image they were bound to be concettists who would hold up the mirror to nature and subsequently load their poems with conceits either copied directly from those in the universe around them or constructed analogously. This is Mazzeo's approach to seventeenth-century poetry: for him, Metaphysical poetry mirrors an analogical universe in which everything has an occult connection with everything else.

Mazzeo has produced an attractive and plausible theory which is very hard to prove on account of the predominantly empirical nature of English poetry in this period and the scarcity of contemporary commentaries on literary theory. There are plenty of programme-poems (such as Sidney's anti-Petrarchan pieces and Herbert's 'Jordan' poems) but none of these hints at any theoretical basis for literary conceits. In fact, it was not until the *avant-garde* had renounced conceits that Englishmen like Dryden and Addison finally got around to writing discursively about them, and then it was too late to do the job sympathetically. Things were different in Italy, where speculation about conceits and their place in a general theory of wit was well established. According to Weinberg, Giulio Cortese was the first to supply a comprehensive theory of literary conceits in his *Avertimenti nel Poetare* (1591), although the first important treatise on conceits was Camillo Pellegrino's *Del Concetto Poetico* (1599), which takes the form of a dialogue in which one of the interlocutors is that great writer of conceited verses Giambattista Marino. The treatise which has attracted most attention recently, however, is not by an Italian but a Spaniard, Baltazar Gracián. *Agudeza y Arte de Ingenio* (1649), a title which Mirollo translates as *Acuity and the Art of Wit*, contains a definition of the conceit which seems conducive to a 'poetic of correspondence' such as Mazzeo supposes to have existed. A conceit, says Gracián, is 'an act of the understanding which expresses the correspondence which is found between objects'. According to May, however, Gracián's *correspondencia* is not a metaphysical notion at all but 'refers to the reality expressed by all conceits' and derives 'ultimately from the scholastic idea of real proportional relations' (pp. 27, 29). If May is right, then Mazzeo is wrong, although one can sympathize with Mazzeo's desire to treat *corre-*

spondencia as an occult term like Baudelaire's *correspondances* and therefore interpret *Agudeza y Arte de Ingenio* as furnishing the otherwise missing metaphysic of Metaphysical poetry.

THE FAR-FETCHED

Far-fetched is a recurrent word in seventeenth-century discussions of the conceit. The Small Poet caricatured by Samuel Butler is attracted irresistibly to 'the hardest, and most far-fet [metaphors] that he can light upon', for 'these are the jewels of eloquence, and therefore the harder they are, the more precious they must be' (and the Euphuistic turn of phrase here serves to remind us that Renaissance opposition to abstruse metaphors was directed as much against Lyly and his imitators as against the school of John Donne). In this instance *far-fetched* has a derogatory sense which was common at the time but by no means so general as it is nowadays. It was, however, a word with unfavourable connotations even to writers notorious for their outlandish metaphors, such as Cowley, who makes it clear in his ode 'Of Wit' that a true poet should never 'force some odd similitude' or beguile himself with 'a tall metaphor in th' Oxford way' (*Miscellanies*, 1656).

> Pride and ambition here
> Only in far-fetched metaphors appear,

he says in 'The Wish', writing on the pleasures of rural retirement and never suspecting that these expressions were to be turned against his own verses, as for example by John Dennis, who complains in a preface to *The Passion of Byblis* (1692) about that very 'wantonness of wit' which encouraged Cowley to 'roam about the universe, and return home laden with rich, but far-fetched conceits' (*Works*, i 2). Here we encounter the standard neoclassical objection which derives ultimately from Aristotle, who says in his *Rhetoric* that metaphors should conform to a mean and be neither too obvious nor too far-fetched (1412^a5). It is a point of view which receives its best-known formulation in Jonson's dictum that 'metaphors far-fet hinder to be understood' (*Timber, or Discoveries*, 1641), but we can detect its presence also in complaints against metaphors which are 'racked' (Jonson again) or 'giddy' (Drayton, *Idea* (1619), ix).

At the same time, others who knew their Aristotle equally well were so impressed by far-fetched metaphors as to argue that you can tell a good poet from a bad one by his ability to handle out-of-the-way comparisons. Hobbes saw nothing to complain about if an educated man wrote poems incorporating 'far-fetched but withal apt, instructive, and comely similitudes'; indeed, the more learned a poet became, the more unusual his similes were likely to be, for the simple reason that 'from knowing much proceedeth the admirable variety and novelty of metaphors and similitudes which are not possible to be lighted on in the compass of a narrow knowledge' (Spingarn, ii 65). Uncommon knowledge breeds uncommon metaphors which are appreciated in turn only by uncommon readers, like the ones Edward Phillips tells us about who ranked Cleveland the greatest English poet because 'his conceits were out of the common road, and wittily far-fetched' (*Theatrum Poetarum* (1675), pp. 104 f.). Here the defence of far-fetched conceits is associated with the defence of learned poetry as a whole, it being generally agreed at the time that only an erudite person, a *doctus poeta*, was capable of producing truly great poetry.

One way of getting our bearings on this subject is to study the section on metaphor in Aristotle's *Rhetoric*, for there we find exactly the same confusion about the value of far-fetched words and far-fetched metaphors as we encounter in seventeenth-century criticism. Sometimes Aristotle seems to condone the remote and the recondite. 'Men admire what is remote', he says, and therefore 'we should give our language a foreign air' (1404ᵇ3) – meaning by that untranslatable word ξένος anything novel and out of the ordinary, anything that differentiates literary language from the

language spoken every day. 'It is metaphor above all that gives . . .
a foreign air', he goes on, 'and it cannot be learnt from anyone
else' (1405ᵃ8): a facility with far-fetched metaphors, it would seem,
is the hall-mark of genius. Even a certain obscurity in metaphor is
permissible because 'metaphor is a kind of enigma', and 'clever
enigmas furnish good metaphors' (1405ᵇ12). In other words, here
is a plausible defence of obscure and far-fetched metaphors, based
on the proposition that if literary language is not only different
from ordinary language but better for being different, then the
qualities which make it different are worth cultivating. Curiously,
the *Rhetoric* also provides the corollary to this argument. In the
course of cataloguing various defects which culminate in a 'frigid'
(ψυχρός) style Aristotle specifies 'the use of strange [γλώτταις]
words' (1406ᵃ2) and obscure metaphors: 'if they are far-fetched
[πόρρωθεν], they are obscure' (1406ᵇ4). Indeed, one of the axioms
in this part of the *Rhetoric* is that 'metaphors must not be far-
fetched [πόρρωθεν]' (1405ᵃ12). Presumably he means that they
should not be *too* far-fetched, because if they are they will violate
the Aristotelian principle of the mean. Ideally, a metaphor should
'be neither strange, for then it is difficult to take in at a glance, nor
superficial, for then it does not impress' (1410ᵇ6). If we are to make
sense of all this, I think we have to conclude that if the mean is the
ideal then the mean in metaphors is the *far-fetched*: on one side of
the mean is the *commonplace* (which 'does not impress') and on
the other side is the *too far-fetched* (which is 'difficult to take in').
It is because Aristotle does not clarify his distinction between good
far-fetchedness and bad far-fetchedness that both defenders and
opponents of far-fetched conceits have been able to enlist him to
their cause. Representative in this respect is Hobbes's *A Brief of
the Art of Rhetoric* (1637). Aristotle says in the *Rhetoric* that 'metaphors should be drawn from objects which are proper to the
object, but not too obvious' because after all 'it needs sagacity to
grasp the similarity in things that are apart' (1412ᵃ5). Hobbes

rewrites this in such a way as to emphasize Aristotle's 'not too obvious' and so argue that the excellence of a metaphor will depend on the degree to which its components are apparently incompatible: 'the more unlike, and unproportionable the things be otherwise, the more grace hath the metaphor' (pp. 173–4) – which is not what Aristotle means at all, but what an admirer of the conceits in Metaphysical poetry would like to think Aristotle means when he defines metaphor as 'an intuitive perception of the similarity in dissimilars' (*Poetics*, 1459ª17).

There is the same confusion about far-fetched metaphors in another influential textbook on rhetoric, Cicero's *De Oratore* (Book III). Bold metaphors wreck Cicero's classification system because they offend against literary decorum but embody the insights of genius. He admits (xxxix) that it is 'a mark of cleverness [*ingenii specimen*] to jump over things that are obvious and choose other things that are far-fetched [*longe repetita sumere*]', and this is why he values metaphor as an ornament which 'gives brilliance to the style' (xliii). And when he says that 'there is nothing in the world the name or designation of which cannot be used in connection with other things' (xl) he seems to be defending the use of far-fetched metaphors. At the same time, however, he is committed to a principle of decorum in stylistic matters and feels obliged to condemn the harsh (*durus*) metaphor which takes us by storm and forces itself on our attention (xli); from which one can only conclude that his account of metaphors is self-contradictory because the metaphors of a man of genius will most likely break with decorum. Quintilian did nothing to remove the confusion when he took up the problem in the eighth book of his *Institutio Oratoria*. He tells us in the preface (23) that the best words are those which are least far-fetched (*minime arcessita*), and goes on (vi 17) to condemn metaphors which are 'harsh, that is far-fetched [*durae, id est a longinqua similitudine ductae*]', ignoring the fact that a few paragraphs earlier (vi 11) he has spoken approvingly of the 'effects of extraordinary sublimity' which 'are produced when the theme is exalted by a bold and almost hazardous metaphor [*audaci et proxime periculum translatione*]'.

All the recommendations made by Aristotle and his imitators are directed at second-rate writers or speakers, who are advised never to take the risks habitually taken by men of genius. The effect of this double standard was to encourage poets to attempt bold metaphors which they knew would be disapproved of by the arbiters of taste, and to do so because those very same arbiters insisted that a writer will tend to show his inventiveness or lack of inventiveness in the way he handles metaphors: if poets were to be denied the use of far-fetched metaphors, how could they possibly be inventive? The confusion in seventeenth-century attitudes towards inventiveness in poetry, which Mirollo discusses in his book on Marino (p. 161), is inherited therefore from Cicero and the rhetoricians who imitated him. As Mirollo points out, Italian critics warned poets against using far-fetched (*ardita*) conceits but at the same time looked upon such conceits as a mark of a poet's inventiveness, so that paradoxically poets induced the admired quality of *meraviglia* as a result of ignoring neoclassical counsels of moderation and fetching their metaphors from remote sources. The crucial question in all this (namely, how *far* might a metaphor be *fet* before one can justifiably call it *far-fet*?) is avoided by everybody, and not surprisingly.

In England the issue was clouded even further by a controversy over the relative merits of plain and ornate styles in both poetry and prose, a controversy which was fundamentally ethical rather than aesthetic. One of the most articulate apologists for the plain style was Ben Jonson, who equated plain language with plain dealing and was therefore suspicious of something as deliberately obscurantist as a far-fetched metaphor. Underlying such attitudes is an English insularity which breeds a wariness of anything outlandish, in manners and religion especially, but also in dress and language.

Puttenham Englished the rhetorical device of *metalepsis* as 'the Far-fet', and said it was used of occasions 'when we had rather fetch a word a great way off than to use one nearer hand to express the matter as well and plainer'; hence the proverb, he adds mischievously, 'things far-fet and dear bought are good for ladies' (p. 193). His definition implies that nothing is to be gained by importing the exotic, because the best is already at hand. I think it not improbable that *far-fet* (as a literary term of disparagement) was used originally in connection with protests against the augmentation of the vernacular by loan-words and scholarly coinages, and that an insular distrust of anything outlandish was transferred from ink-horn terms to poetic imagery as the rudiments of literary criticism were being shaped early in the seventeenth century. Is it not strange that Sidney should complain about 'far-fet maxims of philosophy' and of words 'so far-fet' that they 'seem strangers, to any poor Englishman', but never speak of far-fetched *metaphors*, despite the fact that *An Apology for Poetry* contains a trenchant critique of the Euphuistic style with its surfeit of outlandish similes drawn from herb-lore, beast-lore, moralized mineralogy, and what not?

3
Some Common Types of Conceit

Our increasing awareness of continuities between sixteenth- and seventeenth-century poetry makes it no longer practicable to separate Elizabethan from Metaphysical conceits in the way Alden attempted to do some forty years ago. Alternative categories are hard to find, however, for each set has its own particular limitations. To classify conceits according to subject-matter (alchemical, mythological, legal, astrological, etc.) reveals the enormous range of materials drawn on by concettists, but it is a cumbersome way of illustrating how a concettist's mind works; and to classify conceits by the names of celebrated practitioners (Gongoristic, Petrarchan, Marinistic, Donnean) creates difficulties because many conceits which are characteristic of (say) Petrarch or Donne are not original in those writers, and distinctions between a Gongorism and a Marinism often seem non-existent. My own categories are rather mixed ones, unfortunately. Ideally, I would propose a completely diachronic set, like the present *typological* or *etymological* categories, because these enable one to compare literary conceits without being troubled by such distractions as the nationality of a writer, the century in which he lived, or the literary influences of which he may or may not have been conscious. Diachronic categories are 'constants' in the physics of literature, for a typological conceit will always be recognizable as such whether the maker of it is called St Augustine or George Herbert or T. S. Eliot.

When as much is known about the practice of numerology as is now known about the theory of it we shall be able to study Donne's 'The Primrose' in the context of numerological conceits. Meanwhile, I hope the reader will feel encouraged to supplement the following account with other diachronic categories I have overlooked.

SONNETEERING CONCEITS

These are what usually spring to mind whenever we are asked to distinguish conceits which are 'Elizabethan' and decorative from those which are 'Metaphysical' and functional. Because sonnet-sequences are mainly about love, sonneteering conceits are an alphabet of love, encompassing the experience itself as well as a system for describing those girls whose beauty powered the sonnet industry; and because poets have often found it easier to anatomize a lover's unhappiness than to frame the lineaments of gratified desire, sonneteering conceits were once indispensable to chroniclers of what John Berryman might call 'requited love, un-'. The territory has been well mapped by Scott and Pearson, and especially by John, whose account of *The Elizabethan Sonnet Sequences* (1938) contains a useful appendix in which references to recurrent conceits are arranged by subject.

The Lover's Malady

In externalizing the experience of love by inventing a god who causes people to fall in love (and then declaring everyone to be at the mercy of such a god) sonneteers were able to draw on the Cupid-lore accumulated by classical poets who had invested the god with various symbolic attributes, each illuminating some aspect of that otherwise benighted condition which is known as 'being in love'. Love is a volatile experience, and so Eros is winged from earliest times; it is irrational and unpredictable, and so the god takes the form of a wayward and playfully irresponsible child; love comes upon us with the swiftness of an arrow, which is why Euripides gave Eros a bow; and because one can fall out of love as easily as one falls in, Ovid gave Cupid two arrows, one with a gold-tipped stimulant, the other with a leaden depressant

(*Metamorphoses*, I 467 ff.). Armed in this way, Cupid is often described as a warrior who conceals himself in a beautiful woman's eyes and then ambushes any man who is careless enough to glance in her direction; and because people speak of 'love at first *sight*', Cupid's arrow invariably penetrates the lover's eye before it ricochets into his heart and lodges there. This is one of the reasons why Platonists who regard sight as the noblest of our five senses and disapprove of all emotions which threaten the sovereignty of reason present Cupid as blindfolded, for the love Cupid represents is the kind which ends grossly in sexual consummation and not the higher love which leads to communion with the divine (see Erwin Panofsky's account of Blind Cupid in *Studies in Iconology*, New York, 1939).

Another hoard of conventional conceits was available to anybody who wanted to graduate from the poetry of falling in love to the poetry of being in love. Most of these derive from medieval diagnoses of the lover's malady, the symptoms of which are neatly summarized by Cupid himself in *The Romaunt of the Rose*. Love, says Cupid, is inescapable (1930), a form of imprisonment (2028), a cause of 'peyne and gret adversitee' (2010); it is bitter-sweet (2296) and engenders emotional extremes which make the life of love 'ful contrarie' (2302). A lover finds he likes his own company best (2393 ff.). He is subject to hot and cold flushes (2398), occasionally inert (2408) and speechless (2410), and given to uttering great sighs (2414). He composes songs and 'complayntes' in the hope of pleasing his lady (2325 ff.); absence from her makes him miserable (2420), but to see her and not possess her is an unbearable torment (2457 ff.). Should he get the opportunity to speak to her he is liable to turn pale and find himself tongue-tied (2528 ff.). He spends his days in a state of restlessness and his nights are sleepless, because he either torments himself with erotic dreams which merely prolong his anguish (2568 ff.), or trudges out in all weathers to watch outside his girl's house (2649 ff.). Understandably, his body begins to show the strain, and he acquires the characteristic paleness and leanness of chronic lovers (2684); and all this he endures in the hope of getting from his beloved a favourable glance (2621) or a single kiss (2610). Details such as these (and there are many more) accumulated and formed part of an elaborate rhetoric of love that continued to flourish in spite of the ridicule poured on it by later writers. The parodies we remember nowadays are nearly all by Shakespeare, who had a sharp eye for the *déshabille* of emotionally unbuttoned young men, as passages in *Two Gentlemen of Verona* and *As You Like It* testify. Oxymoron is the rhetorical device used most commonly in the organization of conceits describing the lover's tormented state of mind, for this figure (which unites opposites) is ideally suited to expressing the emotional turmoil experienced by sonneteering lovers, who found themselves subject to extraordinary vacillations of mood. Most of the common oxymora are assembled in the sonnet by Wyatt that begins:

> I find no peace and all my war is done;
> I fear and hope, I burne and freeze like ice.

The conceits themselves are ancient, for the idea of love as warfare stems originally from Ovid (*Amores*, I ix), and the burning and freezing go right back to Sappho (ii). Both occur in Petrarch and later Italian Petrarchizers, from whom English writers were able to inherit a ready-made vocabulary of love. It so happens that Wyatt's sonnet is an imitation of Petrarch's *Pace non trovo*, but the same conceits recur in hundreds of poems right into the seventeenth century. Almost invariably it is a man who expresses his feelings in this way: a woman is simply the beautiful object of a lover's attentions, a creature whose beauty may be praised in the most hyperbolical terms but who is never credited with emotional responses of her own.

A lover is expected to be jealous of practically anything or anybody who is closer to his mistress than he himself is at the moment. The 'jealousy conceit' is already well established in the *Greek Anthology* (V 84, 171; XII 15, 208) and is used frequently by sonneteers who complain at the way domestic animals as well as wholly inanimate objects like mirrors and necklaces enjoy the pleasure of intimacy with their mistresses. Shakespeare's Cleopatra envied the horse that bore the weight of Antony (I v 21), and Astrophil envied not only Stella's sparrow (lxxxiii) but also her lap-dog (lix); and among numerous examples of something inanimate being envied are Romeo's words on catching sight of Juliet:

> See! how she leans her cheek upon her hand:
> O! that I were a glove upon that hand,
> That I might touch that cheek. (II ii 23–25.)

Less soulful lovers had frankly sensual day-dreams and envied the fleas that could 'tickle the pretty wenches' plackets' (*The Tragical History of Doctor Faustus* (1604), 426 f.), or rhapsodized on the beatific experiences of ladies' underwear:

> Blest petticoat, more blest her smock
> That daily busseth her buttock.

Images like this (it is from a song in Randolph's *The Conceited Pedlar*, 1630) incensed opponents of the fleshly school of poetry who campaigned ineffectually with Thomas Brice against filthy writing and such like delighting. Marston concludes his survey of poets who want to be turned into fleas or corsets or dogs by reminding them that only the bestial are willing to surrender their dignity as men: 'For beastly shape to brutish souls agree' (*The Scourge of Villainy* (1598), viii 137). It never occurred to Marston, in his eagerness to see his fellow poets as reincarnations of Grillus, that the wishes encapsuled in such conceits might be deliberately frivolous, even comic; so he was dutifully scandalized at the wish Barnes expresses in *Parthenophil and Parthenophe* (1593, lxiii) to be metamorphosed into wine so that he might pass through his mistress' body and trickle out deliciously through 'pleasure's part' ('Therein he was very ill advised,' quips someone in *Have with You to Saffron-Walden* (1596), 'for so the next time his mistress made water, he was in danger to be cast out of her favour'). Nashe's response is obviously the right one here, and one need not be as squeamish about Barnes's conceit as the Poet and Laureate of the Province of Maryland shows himself to be in John Barth's novel *The Sot-Weed Factor* (1960, II xxi). Such conceits had to be taken in the spirit they were offered and treated as purely facetious extravaganzas open to further witty elaboration.

The Sonnet Lady

When Elizabethan sonneteers talk about their mistresses they tend to describe them in terms standardized by the Italian and French imitators of Petrarch, praising them for their blonde hair, sparkling eyes, lilies-and-roses complexion, coral lips, pearly teeth, and so forth. An early and practically definitive catalogue constitutes the seventh 'passion' in Thomas Watson's *Hekatompathia* (1582): the girl's 'yellow locks exceed the beaten gold' and 'her sparkling eyes in heaven a place deserve', while

> On either cheek a rose and lily lies,
> Her breath is sweet perfume, or holy flame,
> Her lips more red than any coral stone,
> Her neck more white than aged swans that moan,
> Her breast transparent is, like crystal rock....

Every single comparison here is at least second-hand, as Ogle demonstrated in his packed and informative essay on the classical origin of literary conceits, a pioneer study which has now been supplemented in various ways, notably by L. C. John's book. Ogle shows how the most commonly used descriptive conceits were borrowed from the Roman elegiac poets, who borrowed them in turn from Alexandrian Greek writers. English poets seem to have added scarcely anything to the Latin, French and Italian vocabulary of love. Each of the standard conceits was capable of being elaborated in equally standard ways: sparkling eyes have a habit of resembling stars in a heavenly face, and golden hair is more than likely to turn into golden wires which ensnare the helpless lover. A common way of organizing them was by means of a *blason* or catalogue, a formula established in the thirteenth century by Geoffrey of Vinsauf and widely used after Clément Marot produced his much admired 'Blason du Beau Tétin' in 1536. There are numerous English examples, of which Sidney's elaborate 'What tongue can her perfections tell' is probably the best; but Spenser's description of his bride in *Epithalamion* is conveniently short and equally typical:

> Her goodly eyes like sapphires shining bright,
> Her forehead ivory white,
> Her cheeks like apples which the sun hath rudded,
> Her lips like cherries charming men to bite,
> Her breast like to a bowl of cream uncrudded,
> Her paps like lilies budded,
> Her snowy neck like to a marble tower,
> And all her body like a palace fair.

Inventories (even erotic ones like this) can be tedious, although sonneteers seem to have had fewer misgivings than Johnson had on the subject of numbering the streaks of the tulip. One way of varying the *blason* was to pretend that one's mistress had acquired her beauty Pandora-like from various gods and goddesses. Lodge's Phillis, for example, has the eyes of Apollo, the smile of Venus, the feet of Thetis, and various other divine endowments (*Phillis* (1593), xxxiii). The immediate source for this conceit was a sonnet in Ronsard's *Amours* (1552, xxxii), but the 'composite mistress' derives ultimately from Hesiod (*Works and Days*, 70–82) and a couple of epigrams by Rufinus in the *Greek Anthology* (v 70, 94), as I have tried to show elsewhere.

Girls eulogized so extravagantly tended to behave like Chaucer's Merciless Beauty and treat all persuasions to love with cruel disdain (*cruel* being doublethink for *chaste* in sonnet language). Temporarily thwarted, the lover might then reply with a *carpe diem* poem, warning the lady to show him a little kindness (doublethink again) before the passing of the years made her sexually undesirable. *Carpe diem* means literally 'gather the day' and is taken from an ode by Horace (I xi) in which Leuconoë is advised not to indulge in idle speculations on what the future holds in store: 'Reap the harvest of today,' he tells her, 'putting as little trust as may be in the morrow.' Like so many classical themes, this underwent a change when taken over by later poets, for Horace's *live now* became the Renaissance poets' *love now* and flourished as a conceit made famous by Herrick:

> Gather ye rose-buds while ye may,
>   Old Time is still a-flying;
> And this same flower that smiles today
>   Tomorrow will be dying.
>
> . . . .
>
> Then be not coy, but use your time,
>   And while ye may, go marry:
> For having lost but once your prime,
>   You may for ever tarry.

Threats alternate with promises in many systems of persuasion, and any girl who was warned to surrender her virginity before it was too late was likely to find herself being promised immortality in the poems of her seducer. Beauty is transient, runs the argument, but a poem about a beautiful woman will last for ever:

> So long as men can breathe or eyes can see,
> So long lives this, and this gives life to thee.

So ends the eighteenth sonnet by Shakespeare, who made extensive use of this immortalizing or 'eternizing' conceit. Horace claims in his *Odes* (III xxx) to have completed a monument more lasting than bronze, and Shakespeare echoes him in boasting that neither 'marble nor the gilded monuments Of princes shall outlive this powerful rhyme' (*Sonnets*, lv). How tempting it must have been to be given the opportunity of playing Cynthia to somebody's Propertius, Laura to his Petrarch, or Stella to his Astrophil.

The existence of conventional conceits and a number of fairly simple rhetorical schemes enabled many who were devoid of talent to turn out dull and competent verses in praise of their mistresses. Parody was an intelligent way of registering boredom. Some parodists imitated Francesco Berni's trick of pinning conventional conceits on the wrong parts of the face, as Sidney does when cataloguing Mopsa's charms:

> Her forehead jacinth-like, her cheeks of opal hue,
> Her twinkling eyes bedeckt with pearl, her lips of sapphire blue;

and in the play put on by the rude mechanicals of *A Midsummer Night's Dream* the bellows-mender who plays the part of Thisbe speaks tenderly of the lily lips and cherry nose of the dead Pyramus (V ii 338 f.). Another and more popular trick was to invent new conceits and write in praise of the lady's superlative ugliness. The result was a burlesque *blason* or *contreblason*. 'Thy breath is like the steam of apple pies,' Doron tells Carmela in Greene's *Menaphon* (1589):

> Thy lips resemble two cucumbers fair,
> Thy teeth like to the tusks of fattest swine,
> Thy speech is like the thunder in the air:
> Would God thy toes, thy lips, and all were mine.

Sidney's *contreblason* of Mopsa's grotesque appearance shows how easily a composite mistress might become a composite ugly mistress, for not the least of Mopsa's troubles is that she has the chastity of Venus, the foresight of blind Cupid and the lame gait of

c

Vulcan. Similar poems are mentioned in D. L. Guss's study of analogues to Donne's 'The Anagram' (*Huntington Library Quarterly*, xxviii (1964), pp. 79–82); and Conrad Hilberry, discussing later examples in his introduction to *The Poems of John Collop* (Wisconsin, 1962), suggests that poems in praise of ugliness form a separate genre which he calls 'the deformed mistress' (a term he borrows from the title of a poem by Suckling).

In all these instances the aim was to demolish what were felt to be derelict conceits. Other and more creative kinds of parody were possible, however, as we can see in the poems of Donne and Shakespeare. The Dark Lady of Shakespeare's *Sonnets* is a creative parody of the over-publicized Petrarchan mistress:

> My mistress' eyes are nothing like the sun;
> Coral is far more red than her lips' red:
> If snow be white, why then her breasts are dun;
> If hairs be wires, black wires grow on her head.

In rejecting the fiction that gentlemen prefer blondes, Shakespeare is dependent on the conventions he parodies. Powerful feelings may have instigated the poem, but its formal excellences (its systematic debunking of traditional conceits) derive from the thinking head rather than the feeling heart. As parody it is creative in the sense that it ridicules a false convention and at the same time opens up possibilities for a new kind of poetry based on a fresh set of conventions. Sidney's paradoxical encomium of Mopsa leads nowhere except to caricature and grotesqueries; Shakespeare's more subtle modification of the convention enables him to explore a relationship with a woman who is not beautiful by Petrarchan standards, and in this way to widen the scope of love poetry. Donne's 'The Autumnal' employs a similar strategy. Sonnet ladies are always in the spring-time of life, but not the lady Donne here writes about:

> No spring nor summer beauty hath such grace
> As I have seen in one autumnal face.

The theme of autumnal beauty has been traced to the *Greek Anthology* (V 258), and a defence of middle-aged beauty might well have turned up in Donne's *Paradoxes and Problems*; but an awareness of these things should not prevent us from looking at 'The Autumnal' in the context of Petrarchan writings and noticing how novel it must have seemed in its affectionate account of the woman's wrinkled face. Here, as in Shakespeare's sonnet, something new and compelling is made out of the destruction of old and hackneyed conceits.

Because writers were in the habit of parodying conceits in one place and using them seriously in another a modern reader does not always know exactly how he is expected to respond. Many poets, indeed, appear to have operated in an indeterminate area between the serious and the comic, for this was possible as soon as conceits became familiar enough to form the subject instead of the ornament of a poem. Instead of contemplating the *girl* who has lips like cherries and cheeks like roses, Campion contemplates the roses and cherries and makes a poem out of *them*.

> There is a garden in her face,
> Where roses and white lilies grow;
> A heavenly paradise is that place,
> Wherein all pleasant fruits do flow,
> There cherries grow which none may buy,
> Till 'Cherry-ripe' themselves do cry.

Is it our fault that we can scarce check our risibility when a man tells us his girl has a face like a garden? I think not. Such a response is invited here but not demanded, for the poem as a whole is a gracefully complimentary performance. The art Campion displays is the art of maintaining an equilibrium between the metaphoric and the literal, between extravagant compliment and burlesque of such extravagance. It is an art mastered by another expert funambulist, Sir Philip Sidney, in an architectural description of Stella's features which invites us to entertain the idea that Stella has a face like a house, 'Queen Virtue's court' to be precise (*Astrophil and Stella*, ix). *Hero and Leander* is a brilliant performance in this respect because it is for ever guying its own gorgeousness without actually destroying it. Hero has the honeyed breath of a sonnet lady, but literally so, and unfortunately suffers the consequences:

> Many would praise the sweet smell as she passed,
> When 'twas the odour which her breath forth cast;
> And there, for honey, bees have sought in vain,
> And beat from thence, have lighted there again. (I 21–24).

This is far better than saying she had halitosis, which is what an ordinary parodist would have been tempted to say, for the flash-shot of Hero with her lips crawling with bees is just sufficiently grotesque to indicate the presence of irony in the hyperbole. And when we are told that her expensive and elaborate clothes are marked with 'many a stain, Made with the blood of wretched lovers slain' (I 15 f.) we are permitted a momentary glimpse of Hero in a butcher's apron before giving ourselves up to the visual splendours of her appearance. Marlowe is no more committed to his conceits than Sidney is, but like him he recognizes their useful-ness in an Arcadian poetic where the ideal supplants the real and hyperbole is the norm. To recall every now and then the literal basis of a conceit enabled poets to keep the road open between reality and the ideal and to infuse intellectual wit into sensuous enjoyment. The only people who took sonneteering conceits wholly seriously were the poetasters, and they were the people who killed them.

Pastoral Hyperbole

In pastoral elegies from Theocritus onwards the dead man is always mourned by the whole of nature because of the pastoral belief in a sympathetic relationship between man and his environ-ment, as manifest in the identity of sunshine with happiness and rain with grief. A by-product of this 'pathetic fallacy' (as Ruskin was to call it) is a conceit used in the praise not of dead men but of living women, a conceit which embodies the idea that the girl one loves exerts a vitalizing influence on nature, so much so that flowers will burgeon when she is present but fade or die whenever she goes away. Its ritual origin is suggested by the form it takes in the eighth Idyll of Theocritus, where Nais becomes a sort of nature goddess whose presence enriches the pasture and increases the milk-yield. J. B. Leishman calls this conceit the 'pastoral hyperbole' and devotes a section of his book on *The Art of Marvell's Poetry* (London, 1966) to explaining how it was modified by various seventeenth-century poets (pp. 224–37). It developed earlier in England than Leishman seems to have thought, to judge from the evidence of a frequently anthologized sonnet in Constable's *Diana* (1592, I iii 1):

> My lady's presence makes the roses red,
> Because to see her lips they blush for shame;
> The lilies' leaves for envy pale became,
> And her white hands in them this envy bred;
> The marigold abroad the leaves did spread,
> Because the sun's and her power is the same.

Constable's editor, Joan Grundy, cites analogues in poems by Ronsard and Poliziano and other Italian poets, but it reads as though Constable stumbled on the pastoral hyperbole in the course of trying to say something new about rosy cheeks and lily-white hands. For there is a difference in kind between a pretty girl who out-dazzles roses and a nature goddess who radiates vital heat on marigolds: shamefaced roses are bred in a hot-house of sonnet-eering conceits, but it takes an adept at pastoral hyperbole to produce a gynotropic marigold.

> In brief all flowers from her their virtue take,
> From her sweet breath their sweet smells do proceed;
> The living heat which her eyebeams do make
> Warmeth the ground and quickeneth the seed.

The title of Constable's sonnet ('Of his Mistress upon Occasion of her Walking in a Garden') similarly anticipates the later poetry of pastoral hyperbole, for most of the examples Leishman considers are what a former student of his, H. M. Richmond, calls 'promenade poems', poems such as Cleveland's 'Upon Phillis Walking in a Morning before Sunrising' and Strode's 'Upon Chloris Walking in the Snow'. Like the emperor's clothes, the beneficial effect of a lady's *virtù* on her surroundings was not always easy to discern. Suckling watched Lady Carlisle walking in the garden at Hampton Court but thought the place looked no different afterwards, and was surprised to find that Carew had a distinct recollection of how she perfumed the walks and brought the plants into flower.

> I must confess, those perfumes, Tom,
> I did not smell; nor found that from
> Her passing by, ought sprang up new;

but of course, as he confesses later in the poem, he was far too busy at the time mentally undressing the lady to notice anything else. Pastoral hyperbole is old hat to Suckling, although like any other conceit it aroused fresh interest as soon as people started to ridicule it. The faintly insolent opening lines of Cowley's 'The Spring' —

> Though you be absent here, I needs must say
> The trees as beauteous are, and flowers as gay,
> As ever they were wont to be —

rely heavily on an acquaintance with perfectly orthodox examples of pastoral hyperbole, like Constable's, for there is no point in saying what Cowley says here unless your readers are expecting you to say exactly the opposite. Most clever of all is Marvell's use of the conceit in his poem 'Upon Appleton House' (st. lxxxvii), where an indisputable literalness is infiltrated into the old hyperbolical compliment in order to make it palatable to sophisticated contemporaries like Cowley:

> 'Tis she that to these gardens gave
> That wondrous beauty which they have;
> She straightness on the woods bestows;
> To her the meadow sweetness owes. . . .

There is nothing mystical about young Maria Fairfax, although the way the compliment is framed encourages one to think that there is. All Marvell is saying is that Maria is a pretty girl good at landscape gardening. The suggestion that she is a magically endowed nature goddess is encouraged rather by our own familiarity with the tradition of pastoral hyperbole than by what Marvell has actually written here.

HERALDIC CONCEITS

In the thirteenth sonnet of *Astrophil and Stella* Sidney reworks the story of the Judgment of Paris in order to make another elaborate compliment to the daughter of the Earl of Essex, Penelope Devereux. Apollo, called on to declare whether Jove or Mars or Cupid has the most handsome coat of arms, gives the verdict to Cupid,

> for on his crest there lies
> Stella's fair hair, her face he makes his shield,
> Where roses gules are borne in silver field.

Sidney borrows the language of heraldry in order to elaborate the conventional conceit which ascribed a red-and-white or roses-and-lilies complexion to a Petrarchan mistress, and does so for the purpose of alluding tacitly to the Devereux coat of arms, which was three red disks ('roses') in a silver field (or, in the technical language of heraldry, *argent, a fesse, gules, in chief three torteaux*). If the cognoscenti were thus able to identify Stella with Penelope Devereux, sonnet sixty-four encouraged them to identify Astrophil with Sidney himself, for there we are told that whereas Cupid bears an arrow in his coat of arms, Astrophil bears the arrow-head (*pheon*) which is prominent in the arms of the Sidney family (*or, a pheon azure*). The point of using heraldic conceits here, and in Constable's imitation of sonnet 13 ('Heralds at arms do three perfections quote'), is to link each conceit uniquely with one particular person or family, as Shakespeare does in referring to the Yorkist sun at the beginning of *Richard III* (1597 Quarto):

> Now is the winter of our discontent,
> Made glorious summer by this sonne of York.

Others were attracted by the mere novelty of heraldic imagery. Barnabe Barnes seems to have had no particular family in mind when he blazoned Parthenophe's charms in the ninetieth sonnet of *Parthenophil and Parthenophe* (1593):

> Argent in midst where is an ogress set
> Within an azure ann'let, placed right:
> The crest two golden bows, almost near met. ...

Cleveland's Fuscara has an *argent* skin which streams with *or*, and this makes me think that the image in *Macbeth* of Duncan lying dead, 'his silver skin, lac'd with his golden blood' (II iii 112), would have struck contemporary audiences as being magnificently heraldic and not (as later readers have felt) inappropriately pretty for a grisly situation. A more elaborate heraldic conceit forms the basis of William Dunbar's *The Thistle and the Rose*, which was written to celebrate the marriage in 1503 of Margaret Tudor to James IV of Scotland. The rose is 'of colour red and white' (l. 142), partly as a conventional compliment to Margaret's beauty, and partly because Margaret had a Yorkist mother and a Lancastrian father. Dunbar here anticipates a complimentary strategy used by later poets in praise of Queen Elizabeth, the Tudor rose who grew from the symbiosis of York and Lancaster and consequently had 'the red and white rose quartered in her face' (Greville, *Caelica* (1633), lxxxi).

EMBLEMATIC CONCEITS

With a casualness by no means indecorous in a familiar epistle, Horace remarks in his *Epistula ad Pisones* that poetry is like painting in so far as some poems need to be looked at closely and others do not. Out of context, *ut pictura poesis* has been subject to the most famous creative misunderstanding in literary history, for it was liable to be invoked axiomatically whenever it was necessary to justify the presence of pictorial imagery in poetry or lend Horatian authority to a commonplace mentioned by Plutarch, often attributed to Simonides, and doggerelized by Puttenham (p. 218):

> If poesy be, as some have said,
> A speaking picture to the eye,
> Then is a picture not denied,
> To be a mute poesy.

That painting and poetry were indeed 'sister Arts' (in Dryden's phrase) is nowhere more evident than in the emblem books of the sixteenth and seventeenth centuries, which combine moralistic verses with stylized or symbolic pictures in such a way that the picture is intelligible only by way of the explanatory verses, and the pedestrian imagery of those verses is enlivened only by the presence of the picture. Picture and verse were intended originally to be mutually interdependent, although through familiarity with the methods of emblematists one soon acquires the knack of 'reading' the picture without reference to the verse and 'seeing' the imagery in the verse without reference to the picture.

The existence of such reading-habits encouraged poets to dispense with pictures and aim at getting into their conceits something of the vividness and stylized symbolism which in emblem books proper tend to be the engraver's responsibility. This is one way of looking at the tableaux and processions in *The Faerie Queene*. Each character in Spenser's description of the Seven Deadly Sins carries an attribute emblematic of the condition he represents, so that the whole passage reads less like a description of an actual procession than a description of an emblematic engraving of such a procession: Idleness carries his unopened breviary and Lechery holds a burning heart not because they particularly need these things at the moment but because that is how character is presented by the emblematizing imagination. Spenser appears to be alluding all the time to a series of non-existent emblematic pictures which contemporary readers were only too ready to supply, and it is not surprising that *The Faerie Queene* in turn should have become a source-book for later emblem makers like Peacham.

Many emblems contain an epigrammatic motto that summarizes the moral which is expressed more fully and vividly in the picture and the verses. These mottoes could be visualized in emblematic pictures or verbalized in emblematic conceits, which is one of the reasons why Mario Praz argues in *Studies in Seventeenth-Century Imagery* that emblems and conceits are fruits of the same tree (p. 11). Andrea Alciati, an Italian lawyer who invented both the name and the form of the emblem when publishing his *Emblematum Liber* (1531), based over a quarter of his emblems on epigrams in the *Greek Anthology*, and treated *emblem, epigram* and *conceit* as roughly interchangeable terms. Paraphrasing Alciati, Praz writes (p. 18): 'Emblems are therefore things (representations of objects) which illustrate a conceit; epigrams are words (a conceit) which illustrate objects (such as a work of art, a votive offering, a tomb)'; in other words, conceits explain emblems which vivify conceits which explain emblems. . . .

Emblematic conceits offer attractive possibilities to anybody who regards the universe as the Book of God and takes the mimetic theory of art seriously enough to believe that writers ought to imitate in their poetry those morally significant enigmas they encounter in the world around them. In any 'poetic of correspondence' (see page 9 above) emblematic conceits are bound to have a central place because the universal Book of God is written in pictographs, and a major influence on the development of emblem books was a fifth-century work on Egyptian hieroglyphs published in 1505 as the *Hieroglyphica* of Horapollo. 'What are the heavens, the earth, nay every creature, but hieroglyphics and emblems of His glory?' asks Quarles in the preface to his *Emblems* (1635). What indeed: it is clearly the duty of a devout concettist to unfold some of these mysteries and in that way reveal the immanence of the moral in the physical.

Rosemary Freeman gives an excellent account of these matters, quoting at one stage a poem by George Wither that illustrates the emblematic conceit in its simplest form. It is about the sun-loving marigold, and begins with a heavily anthropomorphized natural history of the flower:

> How duly every morning she displays
> Her open breast when Titan spreads his rays;
> How she observes him in his daily walk
> Still bending towards him her tender stalk;
> How, when he down declines, she droops and mourns,
> Bedewed (as 'twere) with tears till he returns;
> And how she veils her flowers when he is gone,
> As if she scorned to be looked on
> By an inferior eye; or did contemn
> To wait upon a meaner light, than him.

And then comes the moral lesson:

> When this I meditate, methinks, the flowers
> Have spirits far more generous than ours,
> And give us fair examples to despise
> The servile fawnings and idolatries
> Wherewith we court these earthly things below,
> Which merit not the service we bestow.

Wither reveals the common tendency, understandable among poets, to value a *speaking picture* more highly than a *mute poesy*, and so he elaborates the verse description in such a way as to colonize the picture; and this is how emblematic conceits managed to pull clear of the emblem books in which they originated. Here now is a more sophisticated example from the opening of Phineas Fletcher's poem on Benlowes (*Works*, ed. Boas, ii 173):

> While pansies sunward look, that glorious light
> With gentle beams entering their purple bowers
> Sheds there his love and heat, and, fair to sight,
> Prints his bright form within their golden flowers.
> Look in their leaves and see begotten there
> The sun's less sun glittering in azure sphere.

A morally significant flower is again the focus of attention, but this time the conceit is far more verbal than visual because the point of departure is not a bunch of pansies but an anagram: if you write *Edward* as *Edvvard* and then reshuffle the letters in *Edvvard Benlowes* you can make *Svnwarde Beloved*, and what more appropriate emblem could be found for a heliotropic contemplative like Benlowes than the sunward-looking pansy (*pensée*), whose yellow-centred blue petals are a microcosmic image of the sun in the heavens and form an occult 'signature' (as above, so below) of considerable value to collectors of divine autographs?

Emblematic conceits are most deeply satisfying when they embody the emblematist's way of looking but are in no way dependent on the engraver's art for their vividness. Among the most perfect examples of purely verbal emblems is the poem by Henry Vaughan called 'The Waterfall', in which both the optical illusion of water hesitating before it plunges into a cataract (a visual effect completely beyond any engraver's skill) and the calmness of the water beyond the falls are evoked rhythmically by the movement of the verse. This is an image in the Book of God which

Vaughan 'reads' as a Christian fully aware that certain falls are fortunate falls: the water's hesitancy figures Everyman's fear of death, but the calm water beyond the falls is a reassuring token of the Christian afterlife:

> Why should frail flesh doubt any more
> That what God takes, He'll not restore?

The possibility that emblematic conceits might in some cases have once formed a private language for the communication of esoteric doctrines is proposed by Frances A. Yates, who believes we ought to try reading Elizabethan sonnet sequences in the light of a book 'on heroic enthusiasms' written by Giordano Bruno and dedicated to Sir Philip Sidney, *De Gli Eroici Furori* (1585). 'Each section [of the *Eroici Furori*] usually consists of an emblem or device which is described in words, this description taking the place of what would be a plate in an illustrated emblem book; a poem, generally in sonnet form, in which the forms used visually in the emblem occur as poetic conceits; and finally, an exposition or commentary in which the spiritual or philosophical meanings latent in the imagery which has been presented both in the emblem and in the poem are expounded' (p. 101). Bruno's Petrarchan language conceals insights into mystical experience. Casual readers note the Petrarchist surface, yawn, and pass on:

> Open, oh lady, the portals of thine eyes,
> And look on me if thou wouldst give me death!

Initiates know better. Directed by Bruno's gloss, they peel off the verbal cortex and discover that the poem is about a death more mystical and high than the Petrarchist cliché reveals, a death which is 'eternal life' (p. 102). What takes place here is analogous to what happened when divine parodists like Herbert consecrated the language of profane love, or when Otto van Veen produced in 1615 a baptized version of the profane emblems in his 1608 collection. In every case the surface conceals the true meaning instead of revealing it. Should we, therefore, read *Astrophil and Stella* as 'a spiritual autobiography, reflecting in terms of Petrarchan emblems the moods of a soul seeking God' (p. 114)? Did Drayton conceive of *Idea's Mirror* (1594) as 'a translation of the *Canticle* into Petrarchan emblems' (p. 119)?

ETYMOLOGICAL CONCEITS

The two main categories of etymological conceits are those which explore the meaning of names and those which presume an acquaintance with the original meanings of foreign loan-words. Both kinds (which I have discussed in more detail elsewhere) are represented in a moving poem Jonson wrote on the death of his son Benjamin:

> Farewell, thou child of my right hand, and joy;
> My sin was too much hope of thee, loved boy.
>
> . . . .
>
> Rest in soft peace, and, asked, say here doth lie
> Ben Jonson his best piece of poetry.

In the first couplet Jonson alludes to his son's name (*Benjamin* in Hebrew means 'child of my right hand') and so gives an etymological turn to the rhetorical device of *antonomasia*, which enables one to refer to a specific person without actually calling him by name; and in the second couplet Jonson displays the funereal wit so common among seventeenth-century elegists by using the word *poetry* in its Greek sense of 'making': young Benjamin was the best thing he ever made.

Name-conceits derive ultimately from the primitive belief that names are numinous and that consequently every *nomen* conceals an *omen*. 'Names and natures do often agree', says the proverb; in which case, exceptions are likely to provoke comment. 'Ah wretch, why was I named, son of a dove?' asks St Peter, in Southwell's poem about him:

UNIVERSITY OF WINNIPEG
PORTAGE & BALMORAL
WINNIPEG 2, MAN.   CANADA

No kin I am unto the bird of love:
My stony name much better suits my case. (ll. 121–4.)

Having denied his Christ, Peter feels that he has not behaved in a manner befitting his Hebrew name *Bar-Jonah* (*Matthew*, 16:17), which means 'son of a dove', and believes that his true nature is revealed more accurately in the Latin form of his name (*Petrus*) on account of its similarity to *petra* ('a stone'). 'Titles I make untruths', he goes on, because he has behaved more like 'a rock of ruin' (l. 173) or 'the rock of scandal' (l. 708) than the Rock of Ages. Southwell is working here in a tradition that goes back to the *Iliad* and forward to *Doctor Zhivago*, a literary tradition in which all names are ironically exploitable 'speaking names' (*sprechende Namen*). Renaissance poets who inherited this tradition often display a fatalistic fascination with their own names ('John Donne, Anne Donne, Un-Donne') but sound a more optimistic note when composing name-conceits for their patrons. Spenser's complimentary allusion in *Prothalamion* (1596) to the Earl of Essex, Robert Devereux, is a prognostication grounded in the discovery of *heureux* in *Devereux*:

> Joy have thou of thy noble victory,
> And endless happiness of thine own name
> That promiseth the same. (ll. 152–4.)

And the title of Ralegh's fragmentary poem, 'The Ocean to Cynthia', derives from a double conceit on his own name and that of Queen Elizabeth, for Cynthia was one of the more common cult-images of the queen as moon-goddess, and *Water* was Elizabeth's pet-name for Sir Walter. Ralegh wants his queen to know that she exercises the same control over him as the moon exercises on the tides of the earth.

The other kind of etymological conceit takes a variety of forms, but occurs most commonly whenever a familiar latinate word is used in its unfamiliar Latin sense. The result may be hauntingly beautiful, as it is in Milton's 'silent as the moon, When she deserts the night' (*Samson Agonistes*, 87), where *silent* is meant to evoke reminiscences of σελήνη ('the moon') as well as of *luna silens*, a phrase used of the moon when it is not shining. Sometimes we are startled by the apparent incongruity of such conceits (when has the moon *not* been silent?) or tricked into believing that a metaphor has got out of control, as when we find Herrick talking about the 'sincerity' of Julia's legs (how can legs, of all things, be either sincere or insincere?). The solvent to such problems is invariably etymological, and all that Herrick is implying in that particular poem (*Hesperides* (1648), xxvii) is that Julia's legs are as unblemished (*sincerus*) as marble, on which *sincer* used to be the hall-mark. The metaphoric thread seems to be broken, but it is not: it is merely hidden in a learned language, as it would likewise be if Herrick had spoken of the *candour* of Julia's legs.

It is of course possible to play the etymologizing game with native English words, as Jonson does in a poem mentioning 'bright day's-eyes, and the lips of cows' (in *Pan's Anniversary*, performed 1620), but most poetymologizers prefer to exploit classical loan-words, where there is likely to be a clear discrepancy between ancient and modern meanings. Of the many writers who display an awareness of etymology, only Milton realized something of its potential when creating the idiolect of *Paradise Lost*, in which semantic change is invested with a moral significance. Faced with the difficulty of writing about Adam and Eve before the Fall – the difficulty of approaching prelapsarian experience by way of a postlapsarian vocabulary – Milton hit on the idea of equating innocence with the etymon and treating semantic development as the consequence of the Fall, thus establishing a series of ironic distinctions between the original 'innocent' meaning of words and their subsequent 'fallen' meanings. The subtleties which result are explored by Christopher Ricks in *Milton's Grand Style* (London,

1963). Milton's Eden is 'a wilderness of sweets' (V 294), but *wild* in the morally neutral sense of 'wild above rule or art' (V 297). It is 'luxuriant' (IV 260) without displaying the vice of *luxuria*, and its streams innocently 'lapse' (VIII 263) or flow with 'mazy error' (IV 239) only in the sense that they meander (*errare*). Eve's hair is 'loose' (IV 497) and 'wanton' (IV 306), but only in the same way that Eden is a wilderness; not until the Fall has occurred does she respond 'wantonly' in our sense of the word to Adam's advances (IX 1015). Looked at from this point of view, *Paradise Lost* is a brilliant though distant relative of earlier etymological conceits.

TYPOLOGICAL CONCEITS

Typology is the name given to a method of scriptural interpretation which seeks to establish occult correspondences between the Old Testament and the New, and by doing so to demonstrate that crucial episodes in the life of Jesus Christ were prefigured covertly in various Old Testament narratives. Originally, the point of doing this was to convince the incredulous that Jesus Christ had a better claim than any other contender to be regarded as the Messiah whose advent had been prophesied for so long. The Old Testament was scrutinized carefully with this end in view, and came to be looked upon as a vast code of hidden prophecies which might be uncovered by the judicious application of allegorical ciphers. An early discovery is recorded by St Matthew, who quotes Christ as saying that 'as Jonah was three days and three nights in the whale's belly, so shall the Son of man be three days and three nights in the heart of the earth' (12:40). In other words, the episode of Jonah and the whale is more than an exemplum of providential vigilance: it is a miraculous prefiguration or *type* of Christ's death and resurrection. Once the principle was established, everything in the Old Testament became typologically significant, and the Church Fathers could set about the business of collecting and classifying types of Salvation, types of the Passion, types of Christ, types of the Virgin Mary, and so on. All one needed was an unshakeable belief that Christ was

> veiled and shadowed in the Old, revealed and exhibited in the New Testament; promised in that, preached in this; there showed unto the Fathers in types, here manifested to us in truths: for the Tree of Life, the Ark of Noah, the Ladder of Jacob, the Mercy Seat, the Brazen Serpent, and all such mystical types and typical figures that we read of in the Old Testament, what were they else but Christ, obscurely shadowed before he was fully revealed? And so all the men of note, Noah, Isaac, Joseph, Moses, Aaron, Joshua, Samson, David, Solomon...

So says the author of *Seven Golden Candlesticks* (1624), Bishop Griffith Williams, in a passage which C. A. Patrides quotes as an epitome of Renaissance attitudes towards typological exegesis (*Milton and the Christian Tradition* (London, 1966), p.129).

These attitudes bear on our understanding of religious verse because devotional writers have long realized the enormous poetic potential in typological lore, both as a formal principle in the organization of long poems (*Paradise Lost*) and as a rich source of material for devotional conceits. After all, the patristic endeavour to establish esoteric parity between Old and New Testament episodes is not so very different from the discovery of similarity in dissimilars, which, since Aristotle, has been thought characteristic of the metaphoric process. Biblical in origin, typological images were prized particularly because they embodied the revealed word of God and so were more 'true' than images drawn from the pagan classics. They could delight with their variety, but all were subservient to the one coherent Christian message, and as such they were invaluable. Chaucer's Prioress could begin her prayer to the Virgin Mary, with the words, 'O bush unburnt, burning in Moses sight', because the bush in *Exodus* (3:2) which burned without being consumed had long been interpreted as a type of the Virgin Mary, who achieved motherhood without consuming her virginity; and there is a veritable catalogue of such types in a poem attributed to William of Shoreham ('Mary, maid, mild and free'), in which the Virgin is described as a chamber (*Psalms*, 19:5), as the dove which brought an olive-branch to Noah, as the sling of David, the rod of Aaron, the temple of Solomon, Judith, Esther, the shut gate in *Ezekiel* (44:2), Rachel, the hill of Daniel (2:34 f.), the village where Christ met Martha (*Luke*, 10:38), and the Woman Clothed with the Sun. Mary could be invoked also in images derived from the *Song of Songs*, such as the enclosed garden or the fountain, the dawn or the lily among thorns, as well as in other types listed conveniently at the end of R. T. Davies' anthology of *Medieval English Lyrics* (London, 1963).

More sophisticated poets who dealt with patristic equations like $x = Christ$ and $y = Mary$ thought it unnecessary to name names, confident in the existence of a large audience capable of enjoying the permutations of x and y without ever forgetting that every x was Christ and every y the Virgin Mary. All was well until the decline of typological exegesis, for when that happened practically every x and y receded into algebraic inscrutability, except to scholars who consciously mastered the cipher, as Rosemond Tuve did before offering us a reading of George Herbert. Her analysis of Herbert's poem 'The Agony' illuminates the working of a typological imagination. Christ is portrayed here as

> A man so wrung with pains, that all his hair,
> His skin, his garments bloody be.
> Sin is that press and vice, which forceth pain
> To hunt his cruel food through every vein.

The image of the vine-press is a traditional type of the Passion. Christ declared himself 'the true vine' (*John*, 15:1), which had the effect of sanctifying every allusion in the Old Testament to vines and grapes and wine: so the story of the men who returned from the land of Canaan carrying 'a branch with one cluster of grapes' (*Numbers*, 13:23) was seen to be a type of the crucifixion, confirmed by the statement in *Isaiah*, 'I have trodden the wine-press alone' (63:3). Herbert's sombre equivocation on *vice* (Christ suffers in the vice of our vices) refurbishes an old patristic image and so stimulates a *nouveau frisson* in readers who are typologically literate. Fluency in the language of types enabled poets to frame devotional mysteries of their own, analogous to those in the Bible but presented far more economically and pointedly. The Jesuit poet Robert Southwell drew on his expert knowledge of 'Types to the truth, dim glimpses to the light' when composing the following lines on Christ's return from Egypt:

> But hearing Herod's son to have the crown,
> An impious offspring of a bloody sire,
> To Nazareth (of heaven beloved) town,
> Flower to a flower he fitly doth retire.
> For flower he is and in a flower he bred,
> And from a thorn now to a flower he fled.

As a priest Southwell is at ease with the typological images associated with Christ, Mary and Archelaus; as a poet he manipulates the types *as images* in order to produce a devotional paradox analogous to the paradox of the Incarnation itself. Christ is a flower, for Isaiah prophesied that a flower (Vulgate *flos*, A. V. 'branch') would grow from the root of Jesse (11:1); and Christ was 'in a flower . . . bred' because the Virgin Mary is the 'rose-plant' mentioned in *Ecclesiasticus* (24:14), the mystic rose without thorns (*rosa sine spinas*). Herod's son, on the other hand, is the 'grieving thorn' mentioned in *Ezekiel* (28:24), 'a thorn in the flesh' of the flower-Christ (*2 Corinthians*, 12:7). Knowing too that the Hebrew meaning of *Nazareth* is 'a flower', Southwell masterfully produces his devotional enigma: 'For flower [*flos*] he is and in a flower [*rosa sine spinas*] is bred, And from a thorn [*spina*] now to a flower

[*Nazareth*] he fled.' Typological conceits, like etymological conceits, are precariously dependent on rather specialized information, and have little to offer readers who think that flowers are flowers and thorns are thorns.

'CONCETTI PREDICABILI'

In the seventeenth century God was well-known for his wit. His analogically structured universe was the work of a mind habituated to *discordiae concordes* and by no means averse to the occasional catachresis; and students of that syllabically inspired masterpiece, *The Holy Bible*, found ample evidence there of the Holy Ghost's fondness for puns and paradoxes. To justify the ways of God to learned contemporaries of John Donne it was prudent to present the Creator as a wit and to expound that wit from the pulpit. The result was a 'witty' or 'Metaphysical' style of preaching which was the ecclesiastical equivalent of Metaphysical poetry, the two being so close in nature that Jack Donne the witty poet became Dr Donne the witty preacher without feeling it necessary to alter his mental habits. Profane conceits were replaced by *concetti predicabili* or 'preachable conceits', the aim of which was 'to inculcate a moral truth by means of a scriptural or physical symbol; the symbol selected seemed so far from the purpose that the mind received a shock of surprise when the preacher appeared to justify its selection by argument and by sacred authority' (Spingarn, i xxxix). As usual, we must turn to an Italian theoretician (this time Emanuele Tesauro) for an explanation of the preaching manner made famous in England by Lancelot Andrewes. The relevant passage, quoted by Praz in *The Flaming Heart* (pp. 209 f.), occurs in *Il Cannochiale Aristotelico* (1655), where Tesauro implies that *concetti predicabili* are an indispensable stimulant to jaded congregations, since 'the word of God appears nowadays insipid and jejune unless it is seasoned with such sweets'. A *concetto predicabile* is the result of collaboration between God, saint, and man, for Tesauro defines it as 'a symbolical witticism, lightly hinted at by the Divine Mind, elegantly revealed by the mind of man, and reconfirmed through the authority of some sacred author'. By word and deed God has amassed a number of discreet witticisms which are spelled out by the Church Fathers and then broadcast from the pulpit by lesser, but nevertheless learned divines. One of God's most brilliant conceits was the Incarnation, although it took a saint rather than a literary critic to see what God was lightly hinting at when the Word became flesh, for it was no less a person than St Augustine who detected God's wit in allowing the Word to become speechless (*infans*) in the *infant* Jesus (*Sermones*, cxc). Hinted at by God and authorized by St Augustine, this etymological conceit on *infans* became an approved *concetto predicabile* available to any poet or preacher who aimed at stimulating devotion by exercising wit. So it is that 'the Word is dumb' in Southwell's poem on the Nativity; and Lancelot Andrewes, sermonizing on the same topic in a passage T. S. Eliot could not keep his hands off (see 'Gerontion', 'A Song for Simeon', *Ash Wednesday*), glosses *Verbum infans* as 'the Word without a word, the Eternal Word not able to speak a word' (*Sermons*, ed. Story, p. 86).

Learned divines less bold than Andrewes might regard it as a matter of professional etiquette to handle only those conceits which were sanctioned by the Fathers, but poets were certainly under no such compulsion. A natural temptation was to cut out the middle-men altogether and gather one's conceits directly from the Bible, revealing in this way hitherto unnoticed examples of what Isaac Walton calls 'Scripture-jests' (*The Complete Angler* (1653), I ii). Crashaw's *Steps to the Temple* (1646) contains a series of 'Divine Epigrams' which is a veritable hoard of such *trouvailles*. In a text from *Matthew* (27:14) – 'And he answered them nothing' – Crashaw discovered a link between the exnihilistic Creator and the self-annihilating Saviour (*Poems*, ed. Martin, p. 91):

> O mighty *Nothing*! unto thee,
> *Nothing*, we owe all things that be.
> God spake once when He all things made,
> He saved all when He *Nothing* said.
> The world was made of *Nothing* then;
> 'Tis made by *Nothing* now again.

Another text, 'Blessed be the paps which Thou hast sucked' (*Luke*, 11:27), provoked the following:

> Suppose He had been tabled at thy teats,
> Thy hunger feels not what He eats:
> He'll have His teat e're long (a bloody one)
> The mother then must suck the Son (p. 94).

As in the case of typological conceits, there is a tendency here to condense and sharpen the contrasts or parallels in order to heighten the wit, the inference being that certain subtleties of the Holy Ghost's were lost on Matthew and Luke but not on Crashaw, whose pointed epigrams restore to the divine *concetti* something of their original crispness. A reader more familiar with poetry than with providence might well suspect the ingenuity originates in Crashaw rather than the Holy Ghost, and reflect on the fact that the secular equivalent of *concetti predicabili* is the Clevelandism. Surely it was Crashaw and not his Creator who anticipated the delights of being suckled by 'two sister-seas of Virgin's milk' and experiencing

> many a rarely tempered kiss
> That breathes at once both maid and mother,
> Warms in the one, cools in the other? (p. 107.)

Divine Clevelandisms are formidable obstacles to our sympathy with *concetti predicabili*, although our understanding of them has been broadened by Ong's researches into the relationship between wit and divine mystery, as well as by Curtius' account (pp. 425–8) of hagiographic contributions to the tradition of scriptural jest. It helps, too, to associate the grotesque element in *concetti predicabili* with Gongorism, for the great Spanish exponent of the conceited style in preaching, Paravicino, was a close imitator of Góngora, who was capable of seeing Neptune's chamber-pots or a urinating cliff where you and I would see nothing more unusual than weeping eyes or a waterfall; capable, too, of pointing out that Christ could scarcely have had cold feet when he was sweating blood (Kane, pp. 75, 78 f.).

THE CLEVELANDISM

The term is now pejorative, thanks to Dryden, although it was first suggested by an admirer of John Cleveland's dazzling conceits, Thomas Fuller, in commenting on the way Cleveland outclassed all his imitators: 'Such who have *Clevelandized*, endeavouring to imitate his masculine style, could never go beyond the "Hermaphrodite", still betraying the weaker sex in their deficient conceits' (*Worthies* (1662), pp. 135 f.). He was impressed by the 'difficult plainness' of Cleveland's metaphors, 'difficult at the hearing, plain at the considering thereof'. Out of context, this might be interpreted as implying that Cleveland spent his time expressing 'common thoughts in abstruse words' (in Dryden's damning phrase). Fuller intended quite the opposite, of course, but posterity has ignored his recommendation and remembered instead the remarkable transvaluation of Fuller's views which Dryden incorporated into *An Essay of Dramatic Poesy* (1668), where one of the speakers castigates an unnamed poet who 'perpetually pays us with clinches upon words, and a certain clownish kind of raillery' as well as displaying a fondness for 'a catachresis or Clevelandism, wresting and torturing a word into another meaning' (Ker, i 32).

A few quotations will show the style of writing Cleveland gave his name to and how it came about that *Clevelandish* is now synonymous with *outlandish*. Here, for instance, is Cleveland on the drowning which inspired *Lycidas*:

I am no poet here, my pen's the spout
Where the rain-water of my eyes runs out
In pity of that name, whose grief we see
Thus copied out in grief's hydrography.

And here is Cleveland's fair nymph in the process of turning down an immodest proposal from a negro:

Thy ink, my paper, make me guess
Our nuptial bed will prove a press,
And in our sports, if any come,
They'll read a wanton epigram.

And here finally is a representative stanza from his poem 'To the State of Love, or, The Senses' Festival':

My sight took pay, but (thank my charms)
I now impale her in mine arms,
(Love's Compasses) confining you,
Good Angels, to a circle too.
Is not the universe strait-laced
When I can clasp it in the waist?
My amorous folds about thee hurled,
With Drake I girdle in the world.
I hoop the firmament and make
This my embrace the zodiac.
How would thy centre take my sense
When admiration doth commence
At the extreme circumference?

Clevelandism is an art of condensation, an art of 'summing whole books into a metaphor, and whole metaphors into an epithet', in the words of an early admirer, David Lloyd (*Memoirs*, 1668). It stands in much the same relation to Donne's poetry as Petrarchism does to Petrarch, for in the mannerisms of Clevelandizers and Petrarchizers alike we are able to detect the manners of another and greater poet. Whereas Petrarchizers codified Petrarch's vocabulary and ignored his spirituality, Cleveland played down the impassioned element in Donne and intensified the wit, perhaps inevitably, for as Levin points out, 'the moment the intellect was called to the aid of the emotional, it became possible to create imagery by formula' (p. 47). Cleveland's formula was one of erudite whimsicality verging on the grotesque. As a decadent (in the strictly literary sense of the word) he made the Metaphysical style the subject of his poetry and treated each poem as an occasion for a display of wit. Metaphysical conceits are therefore at their most vulnerable in the Clevelandism, where emotion is supplanted by intellect and everything is directed to the display of intellectual brilliance.

Dryden's equation of *Clevelandism* with *catachresis* has the effect of loading the case against Cleveland by invoking the traditional rhetorical bias against recondite analogies and far-fetched conceits. The literal meaning of *catachresis* is *misuse*. 'I have supped full with horrors' is an example Miriam Joseph takes from *Macbeth* (V v 13) when defining *catachresis* as 'the wrenching of a word, most often a verb or an adjective, from its proper application to another not proper, as when one says that the sword devours' (p. 146). Imagistic grotesqueness is therefore rooted in a sort of grammatical legerdemain. Hoskins thought *catachresis* 'somewhat more desperate than a metaphor' because it expresses one thing 'by the name of another which is incompatible with it, and sometimes clean contrary' (*Directions* (1600), p. 11), in which case a well-known couplet in Vaughan's 'The Retreat' (*Silex Scintillans*, 1650) might be styled catachrestic:

> But (ah!) my soul with too much stay
> Is drunk, and staggers in the way.

'Only the prick of the point of connection is to be felt in catachresis,' says Tuve. 'The poets expect the reader to shear off irrelevant suggestions with a keenness approaching their own' (p. 132).

Whenever there is a premium on condensation the Clevelandism is likely to be invented, which is how there come to be Clevelandisms in a pre-Cleveland poet like Chapman (see those lines of his beginning 'Love's feet are in his eyes'). Marvell made Clevelandisms look easy:

> But now the salmon-fishers moist
> Their leathern boats begin to hoist;
> And, like Antipodes in shoes,
> Have shod their heads in their canoes.

But they were not always easy to Cowley, and certainly not when he wrote the opening stanza of 'Love and Life' (*The Mistress*, 1647):

> Now, sure, within this twelve-month past,
> I have loved at least some twenty years or more:
> Th' account of love runs much more fast
> Than that, with which our life does score:
> So though my life be short, yet I may prove
> The great Methusalem of love.

It reads like an early draft for a successful Clevelandism. The point Cowley is reaching after in that last line is certainly worthy of Cleveland, but unfortunately the self-styled Muses' Hannibal labours over alps of explication in order to reach it. Cleveland would have got there in a couplet.

4
The Decline of the Conceit

A literary detective called in to investigate the death of the conceit might well suspect that he was dealing with a case of suicide rather than murder. That the cult of ingenious 'similitudes' shortened the life-span of conceits is manifest in the poetry of Edward Benlowes, who ignored his own advice ('Prank not thyself in metaphors') throughout most of *Theophila* (1652) and went on to produce lines like the following (IV lxviii), in which he imagines winter days

> when keen-breath'd winds, with frosty cream,
> Periwig bald trees, glaze tattling stream:
> For May-games past, white-sheet *peccavi* is Winter's theme.

This reads like a parody, but it is not, and it was relatively easy for Samuel Butler to draw up a mock-aesthetic for this style of writing in his character of a Small Poet, and point out that 'when an illustration is more obscure than the sense that went before it, it must of necessity make it appear clearer than it did: for contraries are best set off with contraries'. To read *Theophila* is to acquire more sympathy than one might otherwise have for Sir John Beaumont's view (as expressed in a 1629 poem 'To His Late Majesty') that poetry should contain

> Similitudes contracted smooth and round,
> Not vexed by learning, but with nature crowned.

Equally destructive in the long run was the drift from wit to humour and the subsequent emphasis on epigrammatic pointedness in conceits. Cleveland's verses 'Upon an Hermaphrodite' illustrate this particular tendency:

> Thus matrimony speaks but thee
> In a grave solemnity,
> For man and wife make but one right
> Canonical Hermaphrodite.

So, too, does the following riposte to an older woman in another of Cleveland's poems:

> And yet so long 'tis since thy fall,
> Thy fornication's classical.

By the middle of the seventeenth century, apparently, the secret of maintaining an equipoise between the constituent elements of a genuinely illuminating conceit had been lost to everyone except Andrew Marvell, which means that conceits were enfeebled by various forms of excess even before systematic attempts were made to exterminate them. And it is some of these attempts that we must now consider.

Conceits were jeopardized in the first place by developments in seventeenth-century literary theory, particularly by the notion that conceits are wholly out of place in an epic poem. This is an attitude represented in Sir William Alexander's *Anacrisis* (1634), where approbation is given to Speroni's view that Tasso's *Gerusalemme Liberata* is 'too full of rich conceits' to be truly heroic (Spingarn, i 185). Retrospectively, this looks like the thin end of the wedge, for as a neoclassical theory of decorum began to take shape conceits were excluded from the sublime style and relegated to the low style, invariably in the course of some prescriptive analysis of the epic: anybody writing 'seriously' towards the end of the seventeenth century was well advised to avoid conceits altogether. Typical of the new attitude is Dryden's complaint in the *Discourse of Satire* (1693) that Tasso's poetry is 'full of conceits, points of epigram, and witticisms; all of which are not only below the dignity of heroic verse, but contrary to its nature'; Virgil, on the other hand, is praised in the dedication to *Sylvae* (1685) for being 'everywhere above conceits of epigrammatic wit, and gross hyperboles' (Ker, ii 27, i 256). Here the argument is presented in terms of the Battle of the Books (conceits are not Ancient, therefore Modern and bad), and although it could be answered (and was) that conceits are at least as old as the *Greek Anthology*, the argument was negligible on account of the inferior status of epigrams, even epigrams in the *Greek Anthology*. Nobody wanted to read 'An Apology for Conceits', to use the title of an essay Coleridge once thought of writing (Brinkley, p. 526). Nor was there felt to be any room for conceits in the equally respected genre of tragedy, for most readers would have rejoiced to concur with Johnson that 'the seriousness and solemnity of tragedy necessarily rejects all pointed or epigrammatical expressions, all remote conceits and oppositions of ideas' (*Rambler*, no. 140, 1751). Excluded from epic and tragedy, as well as from lesser genres such as the elegy (see *An Essay on Poetry* (1682) by Buckingham), conceits were not even allowed to remain in lyric verse, for they were felt to be too intellectual to have a place in genuine poetry. 'A poet . . . is obliged always to speak to the heart,' says John Dennis in his *Remarks on . . . Prince Arthur, an Heroic Poem* (1696). 'And it is for this reason, that point and conceit . . . is to be for ever banished from true poetry; because he who uses it, speaks to the head alone' (*Works*, i 127); and Dennis was thinking in terms of the language of the heart when he complained that the lyrics of Waller and Denham had been 'debauched with these modern vices of conceit, and point, and turn, and epigram' (*ibid.*, p. 408). What future could there possibly be for conceits in lyrical poetry when everything had to be subservient to the true voice of feeling?

The effect of all this was to restrict conceits in such a way that it was hard to distinguish them from epigrams and witticisms. Once this had happened, it was easy for extremists to argue that conceits are meretricious and contemptible, infinitely below the requisite dignity of serious literature. Such is the gist of a paragraph in the manifesto with which Davenant prefaced *Gondibert* (1650), where conceits are defined as 'things that sound like the knacks or tropes of ordinary epigrammatists' (Spingarn, ii 22) – epigrams being what Edward Phillips called 'the fag-end of poetry', consisting 'rather of conceit and acumen of wit than of poetical invention' (*Theatrum Poetarum*, 1675; Spingarn, ii 266). True poetry, it was felt, is not dressed to advantage when tricked out in conceits, for 'conceit is to nature what paint is to beauty', Pope told Walsh in 1706, 'it is not only needless, but impairs what it would improve'; and he epitomized his objections even more memorably in *An Essay on Criticism* (1711):

> Some to *conceit* alone their taste confine,
> And glittering thoughts struck out at every line;
> Pleased with a work where nothing's just or fit;
> One glaring chaos and wild heap of wit. (ll. 289–92.)

Conceit and *poetry* became incompatible terms in Augustan criticism, so much so that Ned Softly was type-cast as a poetaster the very moment Addison introduced him as a writer 'wonderfully pleased with the little Gothic ornaments of epigrammatical conceits' (*Tatler*, no. 163, 1710). *Gothic*, of course, is another loaded word in the criticism of this period, and although John Dennis was to warn critics a couple of years later that 'the pointed conceited way of wit was a fashion long before the Goths were either a name or a nation' (*Works*, ii 32), conceits continued to be thought of as literary barbarisms, typical examples of what Dryden condemned as False Wit and Addison as Mixed Wit.

Whereas earlier it had been possible to assert with Italian theorists that conceits are a mode of analogical perception and therefore no less reputable than the logical faculty itself, it now became increasingly common to disparage them for their intellectual flimsiness. In a Cartesian world of clear and distinct ideas there was something quaintly anachronistic about conceits, with their densely evocative irrationality. If good sense were to be the criterion, then conceits made bad sense; they might still amuse, but they could scarcely instruct; they were too intellectual for love poems and not intellectual enough for intellectuals. Only the lowest class of readers, wrote Dryden in his dedication to the *Aeneis* (1697), would 'prefer a quibble, a conceit, an epigram, before solid sense and elegant expression' (Ker, ii 223); and this was the opinion of other notable exponents of solid sense, such as Addison, who canonized Dryden's remark in the sixty-second *Spectator* (1711). The difficulty of trying to write conceited poems in the new age may be assessed from Cowley's *The Mistress* (1647), where the conceits are graceful and witty but in the final analysis purely ornamental, for how can a man believe his poetic images to be true if he believes that truth is the prerogative of the Royal Society?

It is helpful to remember that the Augustan campaign against conceits was provoked by *late* Metaphysical poetry, which is much harder to defend than the poetry of Donne and his earlier imitators, and that the Augustans were far too close to a way of writing they abhorred to be able to treat it dispassionately. A youthful Coleridge might amuse himself with the quaint conceits of Herbert or Quarles, or ponder over the tortuous dialectical ingenuity which enabled Donne to 'wreathe iron pokers into true-love knots' (Brinkley, p. 526), but contemporaries of Thomas Sprat could not afford such luxuries. A famous passage in *The History of the Royal Society* (1667) urges men of sense to avoid 'the trick of metaphors' and cultivate instead 'a close, naked, natural way of speaking' (Spingarn, ii 117 f.). Obscurity became unfashionable, and poets were discouraged from attempting to outdo the outdoers of Donne. Waller's verse was closer to the new ideal than Benlowes' could ever have been; *easy* became the new approbatory cliché and remained so until well into the next century. 'Natural, easy Suckling,' muses Congreve's Millamant. What she means is explained by the critic who also framed the most influential account of Metaphysical conceits. 'Easy poetry', according to Johnson (*Idler*, no. 77, 1759), 'is that in which natural thoughts are expressed without violence to the language', for 'language suffers violence by harsh or daring figures', especially in the case of Metaphysical poetry where 'the most heterogeneous ideas are yoked by violence together'. Some of the taste-makers had the best of both worlds for a time, attacking conceits in critical prefaces but slyly infiltrating them into their poems (some of Dryden's pro-nouncements, for instance, sound like the confessions of a lapsed concettist when considered in connection with his 1649 elegy 'Upon the Death of the Lord Hastings'); but by the early 1700s the new poetry was unwaveringly in line with the new manifestos.

As it happened, the most sustained attacks on conceits were directed not at poetry but at the 'witty' style of preaching, and they supplement our understanding of that shift in taste which resulted in the devaluation of poetic conceits. A representative and accessible example is John Eachard's *The Grounds and the Occasions of the Con-tempt of the Clergy* (1670; reprinted in Arber's *An English Garner* (1895), vii 245 ff.). Part of this book contains a protest against 'fantastical phrases' and 'harsh and sometimes blasphemous meta-phors . . . so commonly uttered out of pulpits, and so fatally redounding to the discredit of the clergy' (p. 265). Eachard worries about the damage done by 'an inconsiderate use of frightful metaphors' (p. 271) which are dangerously remote from the homely similitudes of the Bible. 'But as for our metaphorical- and similitude-men of the pulpit', he goes on, 'these things to them are too still and languid! They do not rattle and rumble! These lie too near home, and within vulgar ken! There is little on this side the moon that will content them! Up, presently, to the *primum mobile*, to the trepidation of the firmament! Dive into the bowels and hid treasures of the earth! Dispatch forthwith for Peru and Jamaica! A town bred on country-bred similitude is worth nothing!'

E

(p. 275); he might almost be talking about the conceits in a Metaphysical poem. 'Fantastical phrases' also form one of the targets in *An Essay Concerning Preaching* (1678) by Joseph Glanvill, who thought it superfluous to 'set off by conceited, fashionable phrases' the truths of the Gospel (Spingarn, ii 276). The common complaint is that witty preachers are gilding the lily. Neither Eachard nor Glanvill, one notices, shows any familiarity with apologias for *concetti predicabili* such as the one Tesauro made. Instead, they present in what one might call Tillotsonian terms a point of view which is analogous to the one Dryden and Addison adopt in matters of aesthetics, and in doing so they helped consolidate the opposition by insisting that the employment of farfetched conceits is an irreverently vainglorious as well as tasteless extravagance.

Consequently, those who disliked conceits did not always feel it necessary to make their objections on aesthetic grounds. Advocates of the plain style in literature tend to be advocates of plainness in everything else and invariably equate ornateness with corruption, especially with corrupt morals and a corrupt religion. This is why conceits have been regarded sometimes as a Papist extravagance, a stylistic disease contracted during periods of monkish ignorance and intolerable among members of a Reformed Church. The argument is stated with fanatical clarity by other opponents of the conceited style in preaching, like the one Mitchell cites who said that pulpit orators should not indulge in 'frothy conceits and tricks of wit' picked from 'the rotten dunghills of Popish postillers and fantastical friars' (p. 154). In a more muted form, such an attitude is held unconsciously or half-consciously by many opponents of the conceited style in poetry. We detect something of it in Cowper's lament that Cowley's 'splendid wit' should have remained 'entangled in the cobwebs of the schools' (*The Task* (1785), IV 725 f.), an image which recalls Baconian contempt for scholasticism; and it is even more noticeable in Hazlitt's remark that Crashaw wrote the way he did as a result of being 'converted from Protestantism to Popery (a weakness to which the "seeing brains" of the poets in this period were prone)' (*Works*, vi 53). Even Coleridge seems to have feared that his nostalgia for conceits in devotional verse was theologically reprehensible, for although he admired some of the poems in Harvey's *The Synagogue* (1640) he had to admonish himself to 'remember Roman Catholic idolatry, and that it originated in such high-flown metaphors as these' (Brinkley, p. 537). Perhaps it is not accidental that sympathetic studies of Renaissance conceits should appear for the first time in an age when the Pope can take tea with the Archbishop of Canterbury.

Certainly it was not until this century that conceits were reinstated as legitimate elements in the art of poetry, and only then in the wake of an intensified interest in the poetry of John Donne. Romantic criticism went in the direction indicated years earlier by John Dennis, and treated conceits as a purely cerebral phenomenon so far removed from the rhetoric of true feeling as to betoken insincerity in the person who used them. By the end of the nineteenth century it was common to wonder why Sidney had used all those conventional conceits in *Astrophil and Stella* if he had been really in love with Penelope Devereux. This is how we came to inherit the notion that a conceit is something frivolous and artificial, vastly inferior therefore to an image. It is incredible that Brown could get along without mentioning the word *conceit* in his substantial book on *The World of Imagery* (1927), except to make one fleeting reference to 'a quaint conceit' (p. 144); and Wells reflected contemporary wariness of the word when he invented the term *radical image* as a synonym for *Metaphysical conceit*, and reserved a different part of his book altogether for a chapter on 'decorative imagery, or the conceit' (*Poetic Imagery*, 1924). Is this the reason, I wonder, why the English version of Mario Praz's *Studi sul Concettismo* (1934) was published in 1939 as *Studies in*

Seventeenth-Century Imagery, despite the fact that it deals with the relationship between emblems and conceits? Perhaps *conceit* would not be the poor relation of *image* if Ezra Pound had been able to christen H.D.'s poems *concettist* instead of *imagiste*, although even the kudos of a Concettist Movement in modern poetry would scarcely have cleansed *conceit* entirely of two-and-a-half centuries of opprobrium. But let us go on using the word until somebody proposes an alternative or set of alternatives which are less forbiddingly complex than the categories in Christine Brooke-Rose's *A Grammar of Metaphor* (New York, 1958). And above all let us keep it simply because its traditional and often contradictory accretions make it such a richly allusive term when handled intelligently.

Bibliography

ALDEN, RAYMOND M., 'The Lyrical Conceit of the Elizabethans', *Studies in Philology*, xiv (1917), pp. 129–52.

ALDEN, RAYMOND M., 'The Lyrical Conceits of the "Metaphysical Poets"', *Studies in Philology*, xvii (1920), pp. 183–98.

BATESON, F. W., *English Poetry: A Critical Introduction*, London, 1950.

BROWN, S. J. M., *The World of Imagery*, London, 1927.

COLERIDGE, S. T., *Coleridge on the Seventeenth Century*, ed. R. F. Brinkley, Durham, N.C., 1955.

CURTIUS, ERNST ROBERT, *European Literature and the Latin Middle Ages*, trans. Willard R. Trask, London, 1953.

DENNIS, JOHN, *The Critical Works of John Dennis*, ed. E. N. Hooker, 2 vols., Baltimore, 1943.

DRYDEN, JOHN, *Essays of John Dryden*, ed. W. P. Ker, 2 vols., Oxford, 1900.

DUNCAN, JOSEPH E., *The Revival of Metaphysical Poetry*, Minneapolis, 1959.

FREEMAN, ROSEMARY, *English Emblem Books*, London, 1948.

HALIO, J. L., 'The Metaphor of Conception and Elizabethan Theories of the Imagination', *Neophilologus*, L (1966), pp. 454–61.

HOLMES, ELIZABETH, *Aspects of Elizabethan Imagery*, Oxford, 1929.

HOSKINS, JOHN, *Directions for Speech and Style* [c. 1600], ed. Hoyt H. Hudson, Princeton, 1935.

JOHN, LISLE CECIL, *The Elizabethan Sonnet Sequences: Studies in Conventional Conceits*, New York, 1938. The best study of sonneteering conceits.

JOHNSON, SAMUEL, *Johnson: Prose and Poetry*, ed. Mona Wilson, London, 1950.

JOSEPH, MIRIAM, *Shakespeare's Use of the Arts of Language*, New York, 1947.

KANE, ELISHA K., *Gongorism and the Golden Age*, Columbia, 1928.

KANTOROWICZ, E. H., 'The Sovereignty of the Artist: a Note on Legal Maxims and Renaissance Theories of Art', in *Selected Studies*, New York, 1965, pp. 352–65.

LEA, KATHLEEN M., 'Conceits', *Modern Language Review*, xx (1925), pp. 389–406.

LEVIN, HARRY, 'John Cleveland and the Conceit', *Criterion*, xiv (1934), pp. 40–53.

MAY, T. E., 'Gracián's Idea of the *Concepto*', *Hispanic Review*, xviii (1950), pp. 15–41.

MAZZEO, JOSEPH A., *Renaissance and Seventeenth-Century Studies*, New York, 1964. See especially the chapters on 'A Seventeenth-Century Theory of Metaphysical Poetry' and 'Metaphysical Poetry and the Poetic of Correspondence'.

MIROLLO, JAMES V., *The Poet of the Marvelous: Giambattista Marino*, New York, 1963, pp. 115–208: 'The Marinesque Style'.

MITCHELL, W. FRASER, *English Pulpit Oratory: A Study of Its Literary Aspects*, London, 1932, pp. 148–94: 'Andrewes, the "Witty" Preachers, and Donne'.

NETHERCOT, ARTHUR H., 'The Reputation of the "Metaphysical Poets" during the Seventeenth Century', *Journal of English and Germanic Philology*, xxiii (1924), pp. 173–98.

NETHERCOT, ARTHUR H., 'The Reputation of the "Metaphysical Poets" during the Age of Pope', *Philological Quarterly*, iv (1925), pp. 161–79.

NETHERCOT, ARTHUR H., 'The Reputation of the "Metaphysical Poets" during the Age of Johnson and the "Romantic Revival"', *Studies in Philology*, xxii (1925), pp. 81–132.

OGLE, M. B., 'The Classical Origin and Tradition of Literary Conceits', *American Journal of Philology*, xxxiv (1913), pp. 125–52.

ONG, WALTER J., 'Wit and Mystery: A Revaluation in Medieval Latin Hymnody', *Speculum*, xxii (1947), pp. 310–41.

PEARSON, LU EMILY, *Elizabethan Love Conventions*, Berkeley, 1933.

POTTER, G. R., 'A Protest against the Term *Conceit*', *Philological Quarterly*, xx (1941), pp. 474–83.

PRAZ, MARIO, *Studies in Seventeenth-Century Imagery*, 2 vols., London, 1939, 1947. See especially the first chapter: 'Emblem, Device, Epigram, Conceit'.

PRAZ, MARIO, 'The Flaming Heart: Richard Crashaw and the Baroque', in *The Flaming Heart*, New York, 1958, pp. 204–63.

PUTTENHAM, GEORGE, *The Art of English Poesy* [1589], ed. Edward Arber, London, 1869.

RICHMOND, H. M., *The School of Love: The Evolution of the Stuart Love Lyric*, Princeton, 1964.

ROSSKY, WILLIAM, 'Imagination in the English Renaissance: Psychology and Poetic', *Studies in the Renaissance*, v (1958), pp. 49–74.

RUTHVEN, K. K., 'The Composite Mistress', *AUMLA*, no. 26 (1966), pp. 198–214.

RUTHVEN, K. K., 'The Poet as Etymologist', *Critical Quarterly*, xi (1969), pp. 9–37.

SCOTT, JANET G., *Les Sonnets Elizabéthains*, Paris, 1929.

SIDNEY, PHILIP, *An Apology for Poetry*, ed. Geoffrey Shepherd, London, 1965.

SPINGARN, J. E. (ed.), *Critical Essays of the Seventeenth Century*, 3 vols., Oxford, 1908.

TUVE, ROSEMOND, *Elizabethan and Metaphysical Imagery*, Chicago, 1947.

TUVE, ROSEMOND, *A Reading of George Herbert*, London, 1952.

USTICK, W. LEE, and HUDSON, HOYT H., 'Wit, "Mixt Wit", and the Bee in Amber', *Huntington Library Bulletin*, no. 8 (1935), pp. 102–30.

WARNKE, FRANK J., and PREMINGER, ALEX, 'Conceit', in *Encyclopedia of Poetry and Poetics*, ed. Alex Preminger, *et al.*, Princeton, 1965.

WATSON, GEORGE, 'Hobbes and the Metaphysical Conceit', *Journal of the History of Ideas*, xvi (1955), pp. 558–62. See also the reply by Theodore M. Gang, *ibid.*, xvii (1956), pp. 418–21.

WEBBE WILLIAM, *A Discourse of English Poetry* [1586], ed. Edward Arber, London, 1871.

WEINBERG, BERNARD, *A History of Literary Criticism in the Italian Renaissance*, 2 vols., Chicago, 1961.

WELLS, HENRY W., *Poetic Imagery: Illustrated from Elizabethan Literature*, New York, 1924.

WILLIAMSON, GEORGE, *The Donne Tradition*, Cambridge, Mass., 1930. Part of chapter 4 is on 'The Conceit'.

YATES, FRANCES A., 'The Emblematic Conceit in Giordano Bruno's *De Gli Eroici Furori* and in the Elizabethan Sonnet Sequences', *Journal of the Warburg and Courtauld Institutes*, vi (1943), pp. 101–21.

Index

Index